THE SPENCERS OF AMBERSON AVENUE

Michael P. Weber

Peter N. Stearns

Editors

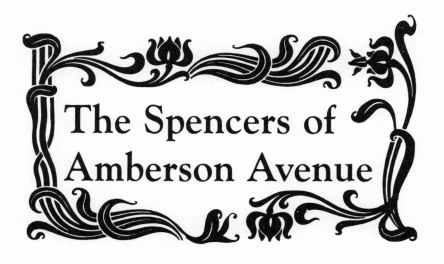

The Spencers of Amberson Avenue

A TURN-OF-THE-CENTURY MEMOIR

Ethel Spencer

Photographs by Charles Hart Spencer

UNIVERSITY OF PITTSBURGH PRESS

Published by the University of Pittsburgh Press, Pittsburgh, Pa., 15260
Feffer and Simons, Inc., London
Manufactured in the United States of America
Revised edition

Library of Congress Cataloging in Publication Data

Spencer, Ethel.
  The Spencers of Amberson Avenue.

  Includes index.
  1. Spencer, Ethel. 2. Spencer family. 3. Pittsburgh (Pa.)—Social life and customs. 4. Pittsburgh (Pa.)—Biography. I. Weber, Michael P. II. Stearns, Peter N. III. Title.
F159.P653S657   1983   974.8'8604'0922   83-47827
ISBN 0-8229-3487-6
ISBN 0-8229-5356-0 (pbk.)

Chapter title decorations are from *Pictorial Archive of Printer's Ornaments from the Renaissance to the 20th Century,* selected by Carol Belanger Grafton (New York: Dover Publications, Inc., 1980).

To Dear Kate

At whose urging this memoir was written

Contents

Illustrations

The Spencer family photographs follow pages 7, 18, 38, 52, 70, 100, 122.

Acknowledgments

The editors wish to acknowledge the important role of Elizabeth Ranney, Ethel Spencer's niece. She first recognized the value of this remarkable memoir and called it to our attention. During the editing process she served as an important source of information. Her penetrating questions regarding our interpretations of the Spencer family greatly improved the Introduction. We also thank the members of the Spencer family, especially Mrs. Elizabeth Spencer Blue, for their willingness to share their family experiences with outsiders. We are all indebted to them.

With a few exceptions, such as those dated after 1912, all the photographs in the text were taken by Charles Hart Spencer. They come from the family collection, kindly made available through the generosity of Elizabeth Ranney, Mrs. Charles H. Spencer, Jr., and Anne Spencer. The captions are adapted from those written by Ethel Spencer.

Introduction

Ethel Spencer wrote this book in 1959, as a memento of the treasured growing-up years she shared with her two brothers and four sisters in the prosperous Shadyside section of Pittsburgh. Her story covers the early 1890s to about 1910, the heyday, at least as we like to recall it, of uncomplicated middle-class life. The Spencer family had a solid merchant and professional background, with store owners on the paternal side and a prominent judge on the maternal. Staunchly Presbyterian, the family leavened a White Anglo-Saxon Protestant heritage with German ancestry. It used its prosperity to provide a solid family home, family-centered leisure, and respectable training for the children.

Ethel Spencer's memoir was intended for family members only. A typescript copy was presented to each of the author's brothers and sisters, illustrated with the abundant photographs which their father had taken during their childhood years.

The book has a number of advantages as a family memoir. It is clearly written, as befits the English professor which the author had become, without being academic. It is observant on a host of features of daily life at the turn of the century. It is not overly sentimentalized, save perhaps for a few passages which are themselves revealing. The result of clear prose and clear-headed observation is a fascinating insight into one kind of urban life of three generations ago.

The account can of course serve to provide historical context for a portion of Pittsburgh that is still elegant and proud of its identity.

But the book also serves as a way of penetrating an important aspect of urban life more generally, in a period when Pittsburgh was showing its muscle as a manufacturing center. Relatedly, the book opens a window on a social group—the middle class—that we know was important, even quietly powerful, but which too often stands silent or stereotyped as we rush toward the greater glamour of the robber barons or their immigrant workers.

In 1907, the editors of the famous *Pittsburgh Survey* described the city as one of extreme contrasts between two existing social classes. "Certainly no community before in America or Europe," Paul Kellogg lamented, "has ever had such a surplus and never before has a great community applied what it had so meagerly to the rational purposes of life."

Through six volumes the contributors to the survey chronicled the underside of industrial life. After spending two years in Pittsburgh analyzing the blue-collar world, they revealed the abject poverty of the Slavic families in Homestead, the filth of open sewerage in the "lower rows" of the central city, the disease-ridden overcrowded company housing provided by the steel companies in "Painter's Row" on the South Side, and widespread vice and crime operating with the consent of the city bosses. Two volumes reporting on the horrible working conditions identified appallingly high injury and death rates, the physical toll of the twelve-hour working day, and the mental anguish of trying to support a family on deprivation wages.

The analysis in the *Pittsburgh Survey*, while detailed and penetrating, actually revealed little new information about life in industrial Pittsburgh. Three European visitors, Alexis de Toqueville, Mrs. Trollope, and Charles Dickens, noted the plight of Pittsburgh's industrial workers before the Civil War. James Parton, writing for the *Atlantic Monthly* in 1868, provided the city's most famous characterization as "Hell with the lid taken off." Two decades later Willard Glazier said of Pittsburgh's inhabitants, "Work is the object of life with them. It occupies them from morning until night, from cradle to grave."[1]

Those at the opposite pole of Pittsburgh's social structure, of course, needed no social survey to tell the world of their station in life. As America's leading industrial city, Pittsburgh probably contained more millionaires than any metropolitan area except New York, Boston, or Philadelphia. The activities of the Mellons, Henry Clay Frick, George Westinghouse, William Thaw and his tragic son, Harry K., Henry Heinz and, of course, Andrew Carnegie were reported upon regularly by the local and national press. The extravagance of their homes, their social events, and their frequent vacations abroad seemed to underscore the notion of Pittsburgh as a city of social extremes.

And yet, the picture of Pittsburgh as a city populated by aristocrats and serfs is as inaccurate as its depiction as a city constantly engulfed in a pall of smoke and soot. Beneath that smoke, penetrated at least occasionally by sun and blue skies, functioned a complex industrial community in the midst of constant change. The life-style of the Spencers of Amberson Avenue and that of their friends and neighbors illustrates that a dynamic, hard-working middle class also existed in the city of steel. The events in their lives—work, play, homebuilding—were repeated by thousands of families in the Pittsburgh district and were as much a part of the urban scene as were industrial accidents, slum housing, and millionaire's dinners. Less dramatic than life at either extreme, the Spencers' story is nonetheless important in understanding the urban and social landscape in America's industrial cities at the turn of the century.

The Spencers arrived in Pittsburgh at the onset of the city's urban and industrial growth. In their lives one can observe, on a microscale, the transition of the American city from a small, rather homogeneous entity in which differences of ethnicity, occupation, and class appear minimal—if in fact they were not—to a large community characterized by sharp spatial, economic, and social distinctions.

Often overlooked in Pittsburgh's impressive development as America's leading industrial city was the concurrent expansion of the city's middle-class, white-collar population. New industries required an ever growing clerical, sales, and management force while ancillary needs provided opportunities to those in commerce, the services, and the professions. The number of middle management and professional workers in Pittsburgh nearly doubled during each decade following the Civil War, and the Spencers and others like them formed an important part of the city's social fabric while managing to escape the extremes of urban-industrial life.

The earliest Spencers in Pittsburgh engaged in small commercial ventures and lived within walking distance of the central city. This area, encompassing no more than four square miles, contained a mixture of commercial, industrial, and residential activities. While small residential sectors could be identified, the spatial distinctions were minimal. Rapid industrial and economic growth, coupled with new modes of transportation, however, brought important changes to Pittsburgh. Shifting population densities, increased land costs, and commercial building construction made the central city less desirable for residential use. Families who could afford to do so began seeking alternatives to inner-city living and the Spencers were no exception. Judge Acheson, Mrs. Spencer's father, was among the first to leave the city, moving to fashionable Allegheny City shortly after the Civil War. Just across the Allegheny River from the central core, the area became one of the city's first residential suburbs. Served by an expanding horse trolley network, it combined the amenities of suburban life with the advantages of rapid accessibility to the city. The proximity of the area, however, soon led to its decline. As neighborhood densities increased, it became less desirable, and many residents, Judge Acheson among them, sought more distantly located suburbs. In 1877 he moved his family to a newly erected house at 832 Amberson Avenue in Pittsburgh's East End. During the next two decades, Judge Acheson created a small family cluster by building houses in the immediate vicinity for several of his children. One son, George, resided at 834 Amberson, next door to his father. Another son, Marcus Jr., was installed at 5131 Pembroke Place (originally Dahlia Street), less than a block away from the Acheson estate. Daughter Mary moved into her new house at 719 Amberson, a few years after her marriage to Charles Hart Spencer.

The Spencer house, like all the others, was carefully designed for comfort and style. According to the architect's specifications, "all the materials shall be the best of their respective kinds and all the work shall be done in the best and most workmanlike manner and in strict accordance with the requirements of the drawings and specifications."[2] The minute details provided in the thirty-eight-page contract between Judge Acheson and George Orth, Architect, give clear indication that this was a house built for a lifetime. Marcus Acheson, like others of his social class, obviously intended that his offspring would raise their families in the environment of his choice.

The family of Charles Hart Spencer followed a route similar, though more direct than that of the Achesons, to suburban Pittsburgh. After nearly fifty years of residence in the central city, the Spencers moved to Shadyside in the 1870s. The rear of the Spencer lot, ironically, intersected the Acheson property along its south side. Thus, in both the direction and the nature of their residential mobility, the Spencers and Achesons reflected a pattern that was becoming quite common to Pittsburgh's middle- and upper-class residents. They abandoned the central city for the more desirable, less densely populated eastern suburbs. They also developed a family complex quite similar, although less elegant, to that created by families such as the Carnegies along Homewood Avenue and the Mellons in the Woodland Avenue–Fifth Avenue sections of the city.

The Acheson and Spencer moves to Shadyside actually preceded the installation of the electric trolley lines by more than a decade. Judge Acheson and later his son-in-law Charles Spencer would for some time to come depend upon the intra-urban railroad for their daily commute to the city. The rural atmosphere of early Shadyside—the absence of paved streets, the Oakland pasture dotted with grazing cattle—illustrates the importance of transportation technology on urban development. Very few workers could afford the time or money required for a daily trip of approximately six miles to and from the city. Blue-collar workers walked to work and would continue to do so until the 1940s. Thus, blue-collar neighborhoods developed along the flood plains near the mills and factories. White-collar workers at the same time began to separate

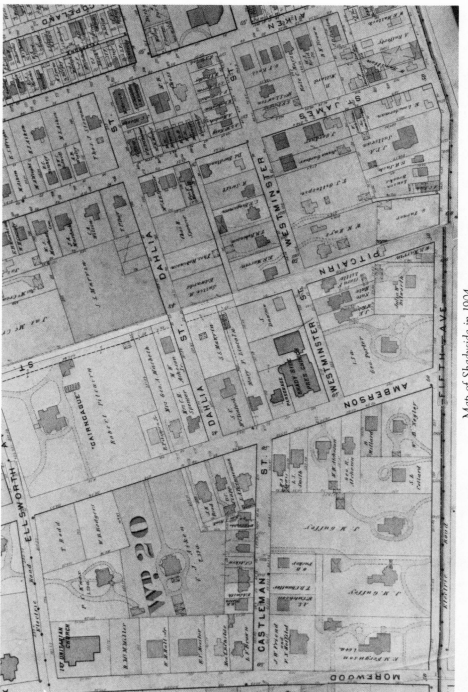

Map of Shadyside in 1904.

their residences from their places of employment. The thirty- to forty-minute train ride from the Shadyside station to Pittsburgh became a common part of the daily routine of Judge Acheson, Charles Spencer, Judge James H. Reed, and the other adult males of the Amberson area. The new modes of transportation inadvertently linked the fashionable suburb with the central business district while, at the same time, isolating one residential community from another. By creating neighborhoods in distant semirural tracts, these middle-class families became increasingly segregated from the neighborhoods of the laboring classes.

The development of a "mass transportation system" in the form of the electric trolley brought major changes to Pittsburgh's East End. Additional families soon joined the Achesons and Spencers in Shadyside. Streets were paved and sidewalks installed. Lots were subdivided and real-estate developers began to speculate in the area. The woods, so enjoyed by the Spencer children, disappeared, and even street names were changed from the pastoral Dahlia and Lilac streets to the regal Pembroke Place and St. James Street. The new residents, however, were strikingly like the Spencers. The household heads of the five immediate neighbors identified in the text included three presidents of small Pittsburgh firms, a physician, and an attorney who headed one of the city's most prestigious law firms. Like the Spencers, three McClintock families—two brothers and a son—formed an extended family cluster all living within a two-block radius.

All of the above families were white, native-born, professional or high-level business families, and all, not coincidentally, belonged to the Shadyside Presbyterian Church. The men commuted to offices in the central city, the women remained home to tend the household and the children. The offspring spent their winters dutifully in school and their summers hard at play. On the surface, at least, their world seemed secure and serene and their values and attitudes, no doubt, seemed safe from outside influences in the increasingly homogeneous world they created.

If the intention surrounding the move to Shadyside was to isolate the family from an unsettled, often ugly world, the Amberson Avenue site succeeded admirably. Certainly the Spencer family seems oblivious to the turmoil swirling about them in this rapidly changing city. The frequent and often violent labor strikes, job-related accidents, and deaths and crime as well as all the other urban pathologies noted by historians of the nineteenth-century city seemed to have escaped the notice of these suburban families. Although not wealthy by Pittsburgh standards, these suburbanities also managed to escape the effects of the long and severe economic recession (1893–1897) which nearly crippled the city. Even the smoke which often managed to blacken Pittsburgh's sky at midday seems to have avoided Shadyside. One early twentieth-century study revealed that the East End was the least smoky section of the entire city.

The male family heads perhaps discussed matters such as these while traveling to and from work or at the office. They all carried the obligatory extra white shirt into which they would change around noon as the city's soot blackened their original attire. They no doubt read of the growing urban crime rate, attributed to so-called foreigners, that was often headline news in the *Pittsburgh Leader* and the *Pittsburgh Press*. And certainly Charles Spencer, as Henry Frick's agent, knew firsthand of the recurring labor problems, particularly the Homestead steel strike of 1892 in which Frick defeated the Amalgamated Association of Iron & Steel Workers and crushed the labor movement in Pittsburgh for the next several decades. Their women and children, however, were effectively sheltered from these hardships of industrial life in Pittsburgh.

The families of Amberson Avenue did maintain contact with the rapidly expanding immigrant communities in Pittsburgh, but the interaction was nearly always transitory and impersonal. The series of immigrant domestics employed by the Spencers clearly reflects the changing migrant patterns within the city. German and Irish servants are replaced by a succession of Polish immigrant girls who, after 1925, give way to two women from Germany. A black laundress—an occupation held by nearly two-thirds of the working black women in Pittsburgh—remained with the family for over twenty-five years.

In each case the Spencer family acted as an informal assimilation agent, teaching the girls the English language, work habits, and certain customs and manners. The immigrants, on the other hand, used their position with the Spencers to enable them to gain a foothold on life in America. Their relatively short tenure with the family reflects a common pattern among immigrant women in Pittsburgh. Upon marriage most relinquished work outside the home. Although only one immigrant marriage is discussed within the text, it seems likely that marriage also terminated the employment of several others. The long-term employment of Minnie, the black laundress, also illustrates a common pattern among Pittsburgh's black women. Only blacks, among all women in Pittsburgh, consistently worked outside the home after marriage.

The contrasting life-styles among the young females who appear in the Spencer household demonstrate most clearly the extreme difference among Pittsburgh's social classes. The Spencer girls obviously worked diligently to live up to the expectations of their parents. Formal education, music and dance lessons, and Bible study dominated their lives and gave order to their daily routine. They were expected to accept seriously the responsibility of "producing themselves." Education, however, was not viewed as a means to occupational fulfillment. None of the children, moreover, was expected to contribute to the financial well-being of the family.

The immigrant females, in contrast, received their "education" in the home of Mrs. Spencer. Assuming adult responsibilities at an early age, their modest incomes often enabled their families to survive. Margaret Byington's analysis of family budgets in Homestead, a Pittsburgh industrial suburb, revealed that laborers in the steel mill received approximately $10.50 per week; a family of four could subsist on $12.00 per week.[3] The $1.50 per week which Mrs. Spencer paid her hired help no doubt went toward mantaining the immigrant family's meager standard of living. An added bonus, of course, was the fact that the help boarded with the Spencers, thus saving their own families the cost of food as well as providing space for other siblings or, more importantly, a paying boarder.

The most striking fact found in the accounts of "mother's

helpers" is that the understanding of life among the various social classes in Pittsburgh appears to be entirely one way. The immigrant girls, after a short time in the Spencer home, no doubt knew a great deal about life on the fringes of the elite world in Pittsburgh. Their firsthand observations certainly uncovered the secrets and rewards of life on Amberson Avenue, a life which must have appeared magnificent by their own standards. Thomas Bell's remarkable novel of immigrant life in Pittsburgh, *Out of This Furnace*, provides a glimpse of the feelings immigrant youth must have had upon entering the middle-class world. In Bell's novel, Mike Dobrejak, a young Slovak steelworker, visits his girlfriend, Mary Kracha, at her place of employment, the Dexter household, a home remarkably similar to that of the Spencers:

> In the Dexters' dining room, in their parlor and bedrooms, he [Mike] saw furniture, dishes, silverware which were desirable and beautiful in themselves and not merely as articles of use. For the first time he perceived how graceful the business of eating and sleeping and entertaining one's friends could be, and how one could be proud of one's possessions, the way one lived.
>
> Standing in the parlor he said after a long pause, "This is the way a man should live."
>
> "It is beautiful, isn't it?" Mary said proudly, almost as though it were her own.
>
> "When a man has this much what more can he want?" . . .
>
> Mary smiled. "You think so? Well, Mr. Dexter would like to have a bigger factory, and he is always talking about getting an automobile. Mrs. Dexter will stay here as long as her mother lives but she says Braddock is getting too dirty to live in, she would rather live in Squirrel Hill where it's more stylish. You see? No matter how much you always want more."[4]

Mary's perceptive comments demonstrate that she knew a great deal about the Dexters, their life-styles and goals. She understands

Mrs. Dexter's sense of duty to her mother and the family's pride in their accumulation of goods. But she also understands that they often remain unsatisfied, unfulfilled, and are motivated by a desire to continue to add to their considerable achievements.

The Spencers' hired help no doubt also knew such intimate facts about their employers. The Spencer family, in contrast, knew little about the personal world of their household help. The South Side, Polish Hill, Bloomfield, and East Liberty immigrant neighborhoods were a short distance in miles from Shadyside, but they might have been in another world. Pittsburgh's middle-class families, particularly the women and children, seldom ventured into the world of the immigrant.

It is tempting for the modern reader to be critical of the Spencers' lack of awareness of the world around them. An almost painful naiveté, by today's standards, permeates the book. One must recall, however, that the world in 1900 was considerably larger than it is today. No radios or television sets existed to recurrently "discover" an underclass of poverty in their midst. The residential suburb, made possible by recent technological developments, further isolated one neighborhood from another. Pittsburgh's uneven topography and rivers, in particular, created strong geographical barriers to community interaction. More pointedly, as the memoir makes clear, the pressures of everyday life—maintaining a certain standard of living, educating the children, transmitting values, and so forth—occupied nearly every waking hour. Life in the Spencer household provided considerable pleasure and comfort but it was, on balance, serious business which provided little time for attention to the outside world. One was expected to make something of oneself, while retaining one's honesty and integrity.

The Spencer family was part of a social grouping as well as representative of a kind of urban environment. The family hovered on the upper end of the middle class, near the very rich but not of them. The Spencers illustrate the kind of life which, more than the doings of the fabulously wealthy, tempts us to recall the turn of the century as a bourgeois golden age.

By the same token, the people and situations described in the book lack some of the credentials we have come to expect from social documents of the past. They are not the movers and shakers, fascinating in their power and tycoonery.[5] Nor are they poor and victimized, revealing the huge seamy side of American history in the Progressive era. They are not even noisily neurotic. On close reading, it is apparent that various personal problems did afflict some members of the extended family, but they were kept under respectable wraps.

The quiet dramalessness of the book's cast of characters is in fact one of the chief virtues of the account. It deals with a major segment of American society—the middle class, or more properly its upper fringes—who are more often assumed than studied by observers of our past. The Spencers fall neatly between the power-wielders of the day and the faceless workers about whom we have been learning a great deal in recent decades. Charles Spencer, the father, was in fact employed by one of the movers and shakers of the coal and steel industry, Henry Clay Frick—and not very happily employed. The family in turn employed its series of servants from various reaches of the working class. The family was nearer the Fricks than the servants. It employed more servants than a typical middle-class family of the day, and lived in a better-than-average middle-class suburb in Pittsburgh. But it suffered somewhat for its pretensions. The poorest family on the block, it made a number of interesting compromises over the children's education and even daily transportation. Not ideally representative, the Spencers nevertheless tell us much about middle-class life.

A portrait of this style of life, in an urban setting still semirural in flavor, inevitably evokes nostalgia, even in a fairly dispassionate memoir. The life was envied at the time, by those outside it who glimpsed it, and we have envied it since.[6] There is no hint of crime. Ethnic groups, among whom the Germans loom largest, are handled via individual servants, often successfully patronized, and otherwise ignored. Children play freely on almost-safe streets, unfettered by detailed, adult supervision during much of their leisure time. Family ties extend well beyond parents and children and, even more than the neighborhood, provide the basic social framework.

Minor but poignant notes of nostalgia sound throughout: The excitement of horse-drawn deliveries. The childhood mysteries of a big, rambling house. Taylor burners—authentic Pittsburgh gas heaters whose flames ran up an asbestos sheet, providing beauty as well as warmth, now illegal in a safety-conscious age. Civil War veterans' parades, when war seemed both remote and honorable. Fresh foods, for people who took good eating for granted. And other points that can appeal to memories or images of a life now past.

Nostalgia is not, of course, the only harvest of a memoir of this sort. Indeed, one of the merits of the account is its stimulation of some assessment of a kind of setting that we too often bathe with simplicity, as a souvenir against our own more chaotic environment. This assessment need not displace nostalgia; certainly, it need not debunk the real virtues of middle-class life in its first suburban heyday. But the assessment does allow additional penetration into family life and urban life in an interesting period of American social history.

From the standpoint of family life, the Spencer memoir enriches and illustrates some existing impressions, while offering a few surprises and unexpected tensions.

The commitment to education is no surprise. This was long a staple of middle-class life, and remains so today. Indeed, institutions developed for the Pittsburgh upper middle class, as the Spencer children were growing up, still thrive in the Shadyside area. Winchester-Thurston remains a sought-after private school for girls. Piano and dance teachers, less institutionalized, come and go, but the pattern of lessons in respectable artistic skills has if anything extended its hold on the urban middle class. Few people raised in an affluent neighborhood like Pittsburgh's Shadyside today will have difficulty recognizing the educational pattern of the Spencer children. Some will also recognize a few of the tensions involved: how far to differentiate girls and boys in the types of lessons required; how to handle the expenses of a securely respectable education, and what compromises to accept when the budget cannot cover everything.

The familiarity of the Spencer family's educational choices should not obscure some of the innovations taking place at the turn of the century. Children were going to school at an earlier age. The cost of governesses, but also a heightened sense that education meant schooling, put the Spencers in primary school four years earlier than their mother had gone, in her own childhood. At the other end of childhood, less surprisingly, a dependent, work-free adolescence was being extended.[7] Secondary schooling is a matter of course, and college an increasingly likely option even for women. These patterns that the middle class was carving around 1900 separated them dramatically from the rest of American society at the time, where semiadulthood came earlier and even childhood schooling was less enshrined.

Employment of servants, like the commitment to education, is a familiar badge of the nineteenth-century middle class. As noted, the Spencers employed more servants than the average.[8] A typical middle-class family used only a single, live-in maid for all work, and even this practice was beginning to yield slightly by 1900. The Spencers had better than average income for their class, and also an unusually large number of children. (Their seven children contrast with an average of three for the typical middle-class family in the Northeast in the 1890s). The Spencer budget suggests some sacrifices—few expenses for concerts and theater, only rented carriages and cars—that reflect the special need for household help. Need may also have dictated special care in the treatment of servants, though clearly there were some passing employees who did not work out, a constant lament of the middle class at the century's turn. The preference for Central Europeans as live-ins suggests interesting prejudices and a willingness to pay above-average wages for the time. The servants remembered for their diligence and longevity reflect the impact of successful maternalism in household management. These servants were trained in some middle-class ways, in a classic process of assimilation to American respectability through domestic work. Servanthood was a key means for rural and immigrant women to "learn" urban values such as literacy, and several Spencer servants went on to achieve their own secure family status. And while with the Spencers, they were clearly treated as parts, if distinctive parts, of a warm household—hence their enduring affection and loyalty.

The Spencers' family focus can come as no surprise. Along with servants, we expect this as in the middle class of three generations past. The Spencers can easily serve as illustration of the kind of family ties many contemporaries believe we are losing, as we bemoan the family's decline. Yet there are some interesting features to the Spencers' family focus, despite its expected qualities.

The Spencers' care in preserving extended family ties, even in using the family to provide welfare for older relatives, may not have been entirely typical of the period. In some ways it reflects patterns which the working class more commonly preserved. Some middle-class families, a bit lower on the social scale perhaps, were developing more rigidly nuclear family patterns as they moved away from city centers at the end of the nineteenth century—or at least so some authorities have argued.[9] On the other hand, the whole issue of extended family ties is often oversimplified even in our own day, for we are not as isolated in nuclear units as some experts try to tell us. In this sense, the Spencer memoir usefully reminds us of the potency of links to other relatives, particularly, in the modern version of the extended family, around the maternal side.

A family memoir, admittedly, easily exaggerates the importance of family, simply by its failure to discuss the whole of adult life. Nevertheless, the extent to which family focus defined the Spencer lives is impressive—or frightening—for those in the late twentieth century who see in any deep loyalties a threat to personal autonomy. Accident or design unquestionably encouraged this familialism. The unusual number of children, at the time when new levels of birth control were spreading even to the working classes, probably reflects unusual family interest. Mrs. Spencer came from a family of eight children, itself unusual, though only five of them had lived to adulthood. The fact that no Spencer children died was still more unusual, though the turn of the century did see a rapid decline in infant mortality that in most families both reflected and encouraged smaller family size. The

Spencers' one brush with possible child death is interesting, in a period when attitudes toward health and death were modernizing rather rapidly.[10] The fact remains that the Spencers had a large brood to contend with, and this undoubtedly heightened the familial atmosphere.

Whatever the special features, the bulk of the Spencers' leisure time—adults as well as children—revolved around family activities. Children's neighborhood friends mingled with siblings in play. Charles Spencer's one principal hobby—granting that his life appears only marginally in these pages—was family photography. Mrs. Spencer's club activities, particularly her service with what is now Chatham College (then, the Pennsylvania College for Women), pale before her family duties. Vacations, a middle-class privilege in the period, were perforce family affairs, dogs and all. Holidays and even the parents' anniversaries became elaborate family festivals, marking the year's calendar just as community-wide festivals once did in a more traditional society.

Family focus relates to two other features of the Spencers' life, important for the period, that are somewhat less expected. They are less explicitly part of our nostalgic image of the past though they can easily be added in. The relative absence of age-grading of children relates surely to the number of brothers and sisters available for childish play. The fact remains that neighborhood as well as family mixed age ranges considerably in play, until the dignity of later adolescence, just as the extended family mingled ages at the adult level. Schools confirmed flexibility for children, by allowing grades to be skipped. The result, nostalgia at least suggests, may have been somewhat wider horizons for all involved.

More significant is the overall pattern of childrearing suggested for the turn of the century middle class. The memoir presents no full statement of childrearing tactics and intentions. The absence of comment on the treatment of infants is unfortunate, particularly for readers with remnants of the Freudian faith. As to older children, some elements of the Spencer family strategy are predictable enough. Mrs. Spencer stressed achievement and good conduct in all endeavor. The Spencer children displayed a vigorous conscience, as in taking responsibility for misbehavior at school. Elements of the household were highly regulated, which follows from the sheer size of the enterprise as well as from our notions of what to expect from late Victorians. The father's presence, particularly, required that children be little heard when seen. but so did Mrs. Spencer's Sunday observance, and elements of holiday ritual.

Yet in other ways, the household was quite permissive. The memoir speaks little about regular or arduous chores, until children could acquire real skills in burdensome activities like sewing. The amount of unsupervised play suggests a confidence in good behavior that did not require regular discipline. The turn of the century was in fact a permissive period in official childrearing advice.[11] Greater rigor would be reintroduced around 1910, and would last until the age of Spock began in the 1940s. In this respect, the latitude Mrs. Spencer allowed may well have been typical. Further, despite our images of Victorian strictness in sexual habits, we are increasingly learning that middle-class families prided themselves on allowing children considerable independence in contacts with the opposite sex.[12] This, too, shows in the dating behavior only somewhat fearfully allowed Spencer girls by the age of sixteen or so.

Ethel Spencer enriches our understanding of the middle-class house as a physical space as well as the place of children in it. Here the emphasis rests on contrasts with more recent middle-class values. Privacy was defined less rigorously than we expect today—with the notable exception of the adult male, who had some definite space of his own.[13] Children shared bedrooms—no great surprise in a family of this size—and did not regard these rooms as centers of much activity beyond sleep. Bathroom space was most exiguous of all. Here, as in other respects such as birth rate, the Spencers lagged a bit behind common class patterns. New middle-class housing around 1900 was beginning to reflect the revolution in family/toilet ratios in which we still participate. Clearly, despite continuities with important features of middle-class family life, the twentieth century has brought significant changes in definition, which a memoir of this sort helps illuminate by contrast.

Dominating both family and household, in life according to the

Spencers, was the presence of mother. The historian must rush to
note some atypical features of the maternal presence. The early
death of Charles Spencer surely reduced his impact on a later
memoir, and even in life his presence was perhaps less impressive
than was typical in middle-class families of the day. Mrs. Spencer
was surely atypical in the extent of her vigor and impact. Her
college education sets her apart from most middle-class women of
her day. Her longevity and enduring impact on her children,
beyond their growing-up years, heighten her visibility in the
memoir.

Nevertheless, several points can be drawn from Mrs. Spencer's
role that go beyond her own unusual personality. She surely lays to
rest any idea of the idle, pedestaled Victorian wife. Historians of
the middle class have long been arguing that this image was far
more myth than fact, and the memoir graphically illustrates the
point.[14] Mrs. Spencer's life was bounded by duty and filled with
hard labor. The range of her enterprise, even counting in the
important work of servants, is extraordinary—all the more given
the hints of distaste for some of the most needful chores.

In other respects, Mrs. Spencer's life as housewife and mother
raises in concrete fashion some of the questions we still ask of
women in the past, after two rounds of twentieth-century femi-
nism. How could she accept such a limited sphere of activity? Did
her religion, her joy in motherhood, possibly some joy in her
husband that Ethel Spencer's memoir only dimly reflects answer
the questions she may have asked about her life?

Without question, Mrs. Spencer wielded and enjoyed real
household power. Disagreements with her husband were handled
by compromise, not obedience. Thus the family divided in its
medical faiths, between homeopathy and allopathy. It divided
religiously, with father allowed a quiet skepticism which was not to
interfere with the way children were raised. On issues where
compromise was impossible, such as college education for girls,
Mrs. Spencer prevailed. Apart from specific issues, the sheer
emotional dominance of Mrs. Spencer, her ability to command
love from each child's entire body and soul, borders on the awe-
some, at least to those of us who live in an age when mothers

themselves question the nature and importance of the maternal role. Again, the balance of personalities may have left the Spencers particularly open to maternal rule, but the power of women in the household cannot be dismissed on these grounds alone. Among students of Victorian society, a school has developed which stresses the family as the first arena of new female power, and this "domestic feminist" approach finds considerable confirmation in the Spencer case.

Which leaves, of course, the interesting issue of the paternal role. Charles Spencer's marginal role comes as something of a shock, for we tend to think of middle-class men as real if authoritarian figures in their families.[15] Charles Spencer by no means ignored his family. His creative photographic work, abundantly displayed in this memoir, reflects real artistry and sensitivity. The carefully composed photographs mark him as a highly advanced amateur. He had mastered basic photographic techniques such as the proper exposure to light, lens selection, and the use of perspective. The photographs he produced demonstrate a serious attention to detail and an obvious concern for quality reproductions setting just the proper mood. Perhaps overly formal for contemporary tastes, Spencer's well-planned portrait and landscape images represent the best of the photographic genre popular at the turn of the century. To the discerning viewer they provide a clear view of family life among the upper middle class and perhaps an inner glance at Charles Spencer himself.

Spencer's choice of subject was not artistic alone; he was surely talking to his family with his pictures. But aspects of his family, including childish nonsense, clearly left him cold. His capacity to convey affection was limited, a charge that is still leveled at middle-class masculinity. Uncertain health as well as temperament doubtless limited his role, as has been noted. He may also have suffered in the family for his failure to achieve the eminence of his father-in-law, a circuit judge. His management position may have contrasted unfavorably with his father and grandfather who had been independent businessmen. This was an important status problem in the corporate world taking shape around 1900. Indeed, Charles Spencer ultimately displeased his employer, Henry Frick, which resulted in his resignation (possibly dismissal) as sales agent in the Frick concern. Unspecified disputes over principle led to the ending of his career. Business problems may have contributed even earlier to his isolation. The memoir gives us no clues, beyond the abundant photographs and the children's reluctant submission to Sunday posing, about his views of his family. He seems to have been in the family, but not of it. Was this typical of the male experience? Historians have been writing of late, as they discover manhood as a valid topic, of a crisis of masculinity around the turn of the century.[16]

The extent to which male and female roles, as illustrated by the Spencers, feed a nostalgia for families past is up to the predilections of the reader. At least the pattern seems relatively clear. The same applies to the final aspect of family life that requires comment—the family as a refuge, or in Christopher Lasch's telling phrase, a haven in a heartless world.[17]

Relying on extended family and upper middle-class neighborhoods, the Spencers shielded their children—and themselves—from huge slices of their own society. This was in part at least deliberate policy. Childhood innocence was carefully fostered by prohibitions on vulgarity, down to the racier valentine cards available in local shops. Family problems, like the uncle who drank, were carefully concealed. Even Charles Spencer's bottle was simply tonic water—an amusing subterfuge which seems to have entered the routine of the Spencer household. Mrs. Spencer may have had active political views before her conversion to ardent Wilsonianism, but political controversy or even comment did not enter family life until the children were grown. Life of the majority of Pittsburghers was simply ignored by the adults and unknown to the children, which permitted naive impressions of the city as a friendly town where everyone knew everyone else.

The point should not be unduly belabored. A family memoir may leave out some real-world concerns that did impinge a bit on daily outlook. Nevertheless, the family's success in cocooning itself in a pleasant world of its own is impressive, given the tensions of the period which the memoir covers. Few comparably graphic illustrations exist of how the family haven could operate, though statements that it should provide an alternative to the dirty real world dot nineteenth-century middle-class pronouncements.

Is this effect to be envied? We clearly wish that our own families were more capable of keeping the world from our gates, and subsequent observers may judge that we are still more successful than we realize. On the other hand, we have dropped some of the more ambitious pretensions toward perserving childhood innocence, so perhaps our goals have changed along with our abilities to use the family as defense. Our discomfort with our own results need not overglamorize the turn-of-the-century alternative. It may help, after all, to have a more active sense of what else is going on.

Michael P. Weber
Peter N. Stearns

NOTES

1. Willard Glazier, *Peculiarities of American Cities* (Philadelphia: Hubbard Brothers, 1883), p. 333.

2. "Architect's specifications for house at 719 Amberson Avenue" (1884). In possession of the current residents of 719 Amberson Avenue, Mr. and Mrs. Francis E. Fairman III. We wish to thank Mr. and Mrs. Fairman for allowing us to photograph the architect's floor plan and for a most helpful tour of the house.

3. Margaret Byington, *Homestead: The Households of a Mill Town* (New York: Russell Sage Foundation, 1910), pp. 180–84.

4. Thomas Bell, *Out of This Furnace* (Pittsburgh: University of Pittsburgh Press, 1976), pp. 136–37.

5. Relevant histories of the wealthy are: Frederic Cople Jaher, *The Urban Establishment: Upper Strata in Boston, New York, Charleston, Chicago, and Los Angeles* (Champaign: University of Illinois Press, 1981); John N. Ingham, *Iron Barons: A Social Analysis of an American Urban Elite, 1874–1965* (Westport: Greenwood Press, 1978).

6. Christopher Lasch, *Haven in a Heartless World: The Family Besieged* (New York: Basic Books, 1979), passim.

7. Joseph Kett, *Rites of Passage: Adolescence in America, 1790 to the Present* (New York: Basic Books, 1979), pp. 173–245.

8. David Katzman, *Seven Days a Week: Women and Domestic Service in Industrializing America* (New York: Oxford University Press, 1978), passim; Patricia

Branca, *Silent Sisterhood: Middle-Class Women in the Victorian Home* (Pittsburgh: Carnegie-Mellon University Press, 1975), pp. 22–37.

9. Richard Sennett, *Families Against the City: Middle-Class Homes of Industrial Chicago, 1872–1890* (Cambridge, Mass.: Harvard University Press, 1970), passim; Michael Gordon, *The American Family in Social-Historical Perspective* (New York: St. Martins Press, 1978), pp. 38–82.

10. Philippe Aries, *Western Attitudes Toward Death: From the Middle Ages to the Present* (Baltimore: Johns Hopkins University Press, 1974), pp. 55–108; James J. Farrell, *Inventing the American Way of Death* (Philadelphia: Temple University Press, 1980), passim.

11. Standard surveys of childrearing advice are: Celia B. Stendler, "Sixty Years of Child Training Practices," Journal of Pediatrics 36 (1950): 122–34; Clark Vincent, "Trends in Infant Care Ideas," *Child Development* 22 (1951): 199–210; Martha Wolfenstein, "Trends in Infant Care," *American Journal of Orthopsychiatry* 23 (1953): 120–30; Michael Gordon, "Infant Care Revisited," *Journal of Marriage and the Family* 30 (1968): 578–83; Jay Mechling, "Advice to Historians on Advice to Mothers," *Journal of Social History* 9 (1975): 44–57.

12. Ellen K. Rothman, "Sex and Self-Control: Middle-Class Courtship in America," *Journal of Social History* 15 (1982): 409–26.

13. Gwendolyn Wright, *Moralism and the Model Home: Domestic Architecture and Cultural Conflict in Chicago, 1873–1913* (Chicago: University of Chicago Press, 1980), passim.

14. Carl Degler, *At Odds: Women and the Family in America from the Revolution to the Present* (New York: Oxford University Press, 1980), pp. 3–110 and passim; Branca, *Silent Sisterhood*, passim.

15. Peter Filene, *Him-Herself: Sex Roles in Modern America* (New York: New American Library, 1976), pp. 77–104.

16. Joe L. Dubbert, *A Man's Place: Masculinity in Transition* (Englewood Cliffs, N.J.: Prentice-Hall, 1979), passim; A. Rotundo, "Body and Soul: Changing Ideals of American Middle-Class Manhood, 1770–1920," *Journal of Social History* 16 (1983), forthcoming; Peter N. Stearns, *Be a Man: Males in Modern Society* (New York: Holmes and Meier, 1979), pp. 96–126.

17. Lasch, *Haven in a Heartless World*, pp. xix–xxiv; Nancy Cott, *The Bonds of Womanhood: "Woman's Sphere" in New England, 1780–1835* (New Haven: Yale University Press, 1977), pp. 197–206.

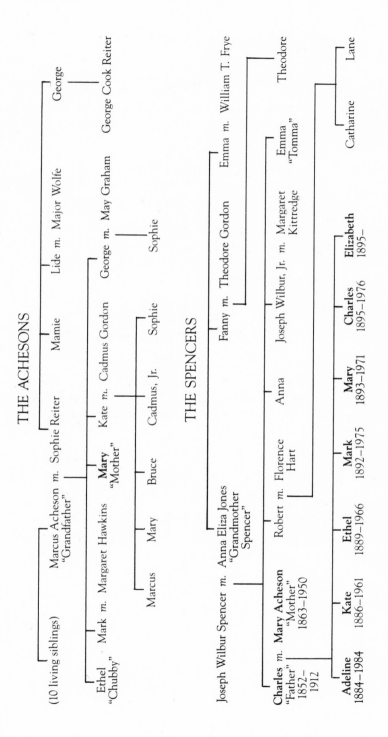

THE ACHESONS

(10 living siblings)

Marcus Acheson *m.* Sophie Reiter
"Grandfather"

Ethel   Mark *m.* Margaret Hawkins   Mamie   Lide *m.* Major Wolfe   George
"Chubby"

Mary
"Mother"

Marcus   Mary   Bruce   Kate *m.* Cadmus Gordon   George *m.* May Graham   George Cook Reiter

Cadmus, Jr.   Sophie   Sophie

THE SPENCERS

Joseph Wilbur Spencer *m.* Anna Eliza Jones
"Grandmother
Spencer"

Fanny *m.* Theodore Gordon   Emma *m.* William T. Frye

Robert *m.* Florence   Anna   Joseph Wilbur, Jr. *m.* Margaret   Theodore
Hart   Kittredge

Charles *m.* Mary Acheson   Emma
"Father"   "Mother"   "Tomma"
1852–   1863–1950   Catharine   Lane
1912

Adeline   Kate   Ethel   Mark   Mary   Charles   Elizabeth
1884–1984   1886–1961   1889–1966   1892–1975   1893–1971   1895–1976   1895–

Note: This chart is limited to persons mentioned in Ethel Spencer's memoir.

The Spencer children had the following careers:

Adeline attended Bryn Mawr College for two years, married, and raised eight children. In her sixties, she started an antique business.

Kate took a secretarial course at Carnegie Institute of Technology and worked for a series of doctors in Washington, D.C., Providence, and Boston, becoming a specialist in arthritic disease.

Ethel graduated from Radcliffe College and did graduate work at St. Hilda's, Oxford. She taught English at Carnegie Institute of Technology from 1920 to 1955; she was head of the Department of General Studies when she retired.

Mark graduated from Princeton University and Union Theological Seminary. He served the Sixth Presbyterian Church in Washington, D.C., and then moved with his family to Great Britain, where he became minister of St. John's Presbyterian Church, Kensington, London.

Mary graduated from Smith College and worked briefly as a physics teacher and then as a medical technician. She married and raised six children.

Elizabeth graduated from Smith College. She worked as a church and then a school secretary in Pittsburgh until her marriage.

Charles attended Cornell University; during World War I he enlisted and served in the Army Air Force. He then became a certified public accountant in private practice in Pittsburgh. He married and had two children.

THE SPENCERS OF AMBERSON AVENUE

Shadyside
in the 1890s

Although technically speaking our branch of
the Spencer family from the very beginning
lived in the city of Pittsburgh, the world of our
childhood was not in the least urban. When
Grandfather Acheson in 1877 moved his fam-
ily from Allegheny to Amberson Avenue, Shadyside was not very
far removed from the farm it had recently been. By the end of the
century, though the streets had been paved and flagstones had
taken the place of boardwalks, the rural atmosphere lingered. A
row of sweet cherry trees on either side of Grandfather's house still
bore fruit of superlative quality—big cherries, almost black when
ripe and richly juicy. The grandchildren swarmed in those trees
during cherry season. Our own backyard had in it two apple
trees and two rather spindly sour cherry trees. When the fruit trees
blossomed in spring, Amberson Avenue looked like an orchard.

I am quite sure, however, that we thought of those trees in terms
of fruit rather than of beauty. Pittsburgh in the 1890s had not yet
learned the value of landscape gardening. Every house stood
starkly in the middle of its ground without planting to hide ugly
foundations or gardens to please the eye. We had some red rose
bushes in our yard, to be sure, but they grew in a round bed that
had no relationship to anything else. There was a round bed of
cannas in another unrelated spot and a long row of cannas between
our backyard and the adjoining cow pasture. What beauty there
was was an accident of nature rather than the result of deliberate
planning.

Yet at some point in the development of the neighborhood

3

someone with an eye for beauty must have made his influence felt, for trees marched on either side of Amberson Avenue from its beginning at Fifth Avenue to its end at the Shadyside Station, mostly quick-growing water maples, but also some beautiful lindens and an occasional elm. The maples dropped innumerable seeds in the spring, and innumerable little trees sprang up, most of which were cut down with the grass. The Spencer twins when very small planted seeds at the end of our property along the Pembroke Place side that grew enthusiastically. Referred to always as Charles and Elizabeth, they helped to shade the street until the Todds, who bought our house in 1950, had them cut down to permit entrance to their garage. In the far corner of our backyard near the Macbeth line stood a big maple known until its death in the 1940s as the garbage-can tree because throughout our youth the garbage can stood beneath it. Why the garbage was placed so far from the house I have never been able to understand, for to carry it to the can through wet grass on a rainy day must have tried the souls of our cooks. But the tree itself was beautiful, and with other trees in other yards it helped to counteract the unattractiveness of unbeautified grounds.

Behind the row of cannas at the end of our backyard a heavy wire fence shut off the cow pasture. I do not believe that cows were common in the Shadyside of our youth, but they did not seem out of the way. Occasionally cattle were still driven up Amberson Avenue from the Shadyside station, where they were unloaded, to the stockyards at Point Breeze, and no farther away than Oakland the present Schenley Farms district was in very truth a farm, with cows cropping hillsides now covered with houses and University of Pittsburgh buildings. Our cows, then, were not unusual. As far back as I can remember we kept one in the cow pasture, and when Sophie Acheson was born, a second cow came to join ours so that all the very young could have home-grown milk. John Organ, Grandfather's Negro man of all work, milked the cows. One of the joys of our childhood was to help him mix the mash, taste it ourselves, and watch the milk spurt into his tin bucket. The milk was carried to our cellar, poured into big brown crocks, and set on the shelves of the double-doored icebox. After the cream had risen, I loved to watch Mother take it off with a flat skimmer. We were able to watch this ritual until about 1902. That summer the cows, standing for shelter under a big ash tree in the cow pasture during a severe thunderstorm, were struck by lightning. I think their spectacular death marked the end of our cow keeping, though the Schenley Farm cows continued to crop the Oakland hillsides for several years longer.

Beyond the cow pasture lay "the woods." The trees seemed to me as a small child to stretch away endlessly. Beneath them the light hardly penetrated, and by day the dim world they enclosed was full of mystery; at night owls hooted. There must have been a dump in the gully, for we found treasures every now and then. I remember only broken bits of china, but they seemed a promise of better things to come. Since the woods extended only from the end of the cow pasture to the beginning of the backyards on Lilac Street, they covered barely half a block, but they seemed to us a forest well touched with romance.

The neighborhood was not nearly so thickly populated then as it is now. On the corner of Castleman Street and Amberson Avenue stood a big square frame house with a mansard roof, long since torn down, in which the Marvins lived during our early years, and later the Brennemans. Next to it was Mr. Clapp's house, in relatively recent times remodeled by Katherine Frazer, and beside it the Reed's big house of red brick, now no more. Then in a piece of property extending all the way to Ellsworth Avenue, with a long tree-bordered driveway leading up to it, stood the Aiken house. Close beside our own house the Macbeths lived, but from their boundary line to Ellsworth Avenue there was only the Pitcairn house—an elaborately ugly example of late Victorian architecture, set in well-kept grounds and protected from intruders by a handsome iron fence. Across Ellsworth Avenue there was the Oliver McClintock house on the far corner, with a cottagey sort of house beyond it. I do not think that Bayard Street had been cut through to Amberson when we were small, but below where it now runs there was only a queer little square house with a mansard roof that Mother spoke of as the Swiss cottage. Above it rose the McKay hill, and beyond that were the Shadyside station and the

Pennsylvania Railroad tracks. On the other side of Amberson Avenue the Albert Childs' house was the only one between the station and the Wood house on the corner of Ellsworth Avenue. Between us and Fifth Avenue was what is now the McClintock house, beyond it the Edwards' house (later the Lincolns', but no longer in existence), then the parsonage and the church. Across Westminster Street I do not remember that there was any house at all except the big square cupolaed mansion on the corner of Fifth and Amberson where the Lawrence Dilworths lived briefly during our childhood. On the other corner was the Negley house, now the Gwinner's, then Uncle George's and Grandfather's houses. Between Grandfather's and Castleman Street only the Bruce house stood when we were very small, but it was soon supplanted by the Smith and Lewis houses.

Castleman Street had, I think, been fairly recently opened in our early childhood. The asphalt used in paving it must have been poor, for under a hot sun it grew delightfully soft. We loved to whirl on our heels on it, and for many years small heel marks in the paving recorded the joy its defective surface gave.

The fact that children could dig their heels in asphalt to their hearts' content indicates how relatively safe the streets were. Ice wagons jolted heavily from house to house, and delivery wagons rattled up and down the streets, but never in great numbers. In the afternoon carriages carried ladies about the neighborhood to pay calls. Occasionally a run-away horse caused great excitement, but on the whole a reasonably careful child could play on the streets without danger to life and limb.

Dahlia Street, though always a threat, was not opened until 1902. Then, although we resented the loss of our side yard and the demolition of the honeysuckle-covered wire fence through which we had climbed into McClintock territory, we thoroughly enjoyed helping to build the street. Spencer and McClintock children were constantly under the workmen's feet. The sewer pipes appeared to have been piled up at the sides solely for our benefit. We climbed over them, walked along their tops, raced along the big curbstones, wallowed in mud—in fact, enjoyed to the utmost every step of street making. Since Dahlia Street opened up the

6

property behind the Spencers and McClintocks, it was not long before new houses began to rise. We watched with proprietary interest Uncle Mark Acheson's house taking shape in what had been the cow pasture, and with only a degree less interest the other houses that soon appeared along the new street. It was not until about 1917 that we ourselves succeeded in selling the two lots father had owned just behind Lilac Street. The money Mother received for this property she used to build the cottage on Coraopolis Heights in which we spent our summers from 1920 through 1934.

I think it must have been fairly soon after its opening that the name of Dahlia Street was changed to Pembroke Place. At about the same time Lilac Street was transformed to St. James Street. The substitution of aristocratic names for garden flowers suggests the general transformation of the neighborhood. By the end of the first decade of this century Shadyside had lost its semirural character and Pittsburgh had ceased to be a big country town where everybody knew everyone else.

The same sort of transformation occurred in the way we got about the city. The bicycle was of utmost importance in our early years; without it we should have been confined pretty largely to the immediate neighborhood; with it we could wander relatively far afield. Late in the 1890s father had a bicycle shed built against the east side of the house between the kitchen wall and the bay window of the dining room. In it there were stalls for the family "bikes," perhaps nine stalls, though the picture suggests seven. The fact that I remember only vaguely seeing Mother on a bicycle probably means that she had ceased to ride before the bicycle shed was built, and I have no very vivid recollection of Father riding his either. In days before I can remember they took long rides in Schenley Park with Adeline and Kate, but by the time the younger children were old enough to take part in such excursions, Mother had too many children and too much to do at home to go bicycling, and Father had lost his enthusiasm. For the children, however, bicycles were the chief form of transportation. We rode them to school, to music lessons, to see our friends; without them life would have been immeasurably narrowed.

719 Amberson Avenue, May 1901.

719 Amberson Avenue (*rear*), 1901.

Amberson Avenue, looking toward Ellsworth Avenue, 1898.

The cow pasture and the woods, October 1901.

Elizabeth helping John Organ milk the cow, July 1901.

The bicycle shed, April 1899: Mark, Charles, George Macbeth, Elizabeth, Fluffy, Mary, Caroline Blackstone.

When a more elegant means of transportation was required, we hired a carriage from a livery stable and rolled in state to our destination. Livery-stable carriages took us to parties, to weddings, to funerals, but they were too expensive to be indulged in often. Grandfather's carriage was almost as exciting to ride in and more frequently available. In bad weather Grandfather sent it, old Dan between the shafts and John Organ at the reins, to take us to school. Though Dan was an old horse, half-heartedly groomed by John, and the carriage was shabby, we felt very grand being driven through streets we ordinarily covered on foot or on bicycles. The sound of Dan's clip-clop always thrilled me, and the crunch of the carriage wheels on snow. Sometimes on Saturdays the older children were allowed to drive by themselves through quiet streets as far as the zoo, and these adventures I remember as sheer joy.

Ordinarily when we had to travel a considerable distance we used the cable cars that ran on Fifth Avenue or the trains that stopped at the Shadyside station at the foot of our street. The cable cars took us to town to shop, the trains to Edgewood to see Mother's two aunts. When cable cars were superceded by trolleys, we dearly loved to ride in the open cars that were put on in summer, but in general street cars and trains were a less exciting way in which to cover ground than carriages.

By 1900 an even more exciting means of transportation than carriages was beginning. The first automobile on our street belonged to Jimmy Reed, and in it each of the younger Spencers had his first automobile ride. Sitting on the curbstone we would watch Jimmy with pleading eyes as he coasted down the Reed driveway across the street from our house, and, nice boy that he was, he took pity on one little Spencer after another and invited us to share the high perch beside him. Adeline very likely had her first ride in Chick Curry's car, for from the time she was thirteen he was pursuing her, usually in an automobile. We younger children used to hide giggling behind the library curtains and watch her climb into his car—was it a Pope Toledo?—through a door in the middle of its back. Later when they had become engaged, and during the early years of their marriage, Chick on Sunday afternoons would fill up his car with Spencers and take us for a drive through Schenley Park and over Beechwood Boulevard. The summer of 1907 when the Currys, the Spencers, and the Achesons took a house together in Marion, Massachusetts, his Packard gave us a glorious summer of motoring. During his own vacation he drove us about the countryside, and when he left he got a chauffeur named John to take over. Roads were narrow, rough, and incredibly dusty, and driving was an adventure whether Chick or John was at the wheel. Toward the end of summer when frail tires had grown frailer from use we had as many as eight punctures in an afternoon. Since each puncture had to be mended then and there, the ladies, enveloped in capacious dusters, their hats anchored to their heads by soft, hot chiffon veils, spent as much time by the roadside as in the car, and the men worked hard for their pleasure.

We were grown up before automobiles became a means of transportation that could be relied upon. Our childhood belonged to an age without automobiles, without labor-saving electrical devices, without radio, television, or aeroplanes. We had a telephone, to be sure, on the wall at the foot of the back stairs, with a handle we ground to summon "Central." Since our number was Bellefield 92, I think we must have been early subscribers. But there was no telephone when the two oldest children were born, for Father had to go to a nearby livery stable, hire a horse and carriage, and drive off to fetch both doctor and nurse. By the time memory begins for me the telephone had become an important part of household equipment, but it is the only one of the great modern inventions that links our childhood with the present. We grew up in a simpler, less complex world than the world of today.

Our House

After Mother's death in 1950 a real estate man came to 719 Amberson Avenue to evaluate the house. Looking from the library room to the dining room he said, "You could put into these two rooms the whole of the kind of house they are building today." Built in 1885–1886 in the so-called Queen Anne style, our house was ugly but roomy. One could turn around in it even when it was crowded. Though spacious compared with the houses of 1957, in our childhood 719 contained barely enough room to accommodate our constantly expanding household. When the family had been completed and the house was occupied by a mother and a father, seven children, and during the early infancy of the twins a wet nurse and her baby, not to mention a cook, a chambermaid, and two regular nurses for the children, it nearly burst at the seams.

During the years of greatest congestion the bedrooms on the second floor were dormitories full of beds and cribs and children. Only three of the four rooms were used for sleeping purposes. The one at the top of the front stairs was known ironically as the spare room. It was spare only in the sense that it could be easily evacuated; when guests came, whichever children customarily slept there were squeezed in some place else. The big room next to the spare room, with its enormous double bed, marble-topped bureau and chiffonier, both of golden oak, belonged to Mother and Father. On Mother's side of the bed the newest baby slept in a crib. Beside the crib a door opened into what later became Mary and Elizabeth's room, but in the earlier days it belonged to no one in particular. Here slept the next-to-youngest baby in another crib placed near the door so that Mother could hear untoward stirrings at night, and an assortment of older children slept in the big double bed. None of us can remember just how Mother normally bedded us down, but in a letter dated September 6, 1895, she describes specifically the sleeping arrangements instituted during the twin's early infancy:

> The wet nurse sleeps on my lounge in *our former* room, with her baby in a cradle at the foot. Marcus occupies Mary's brass bed, and Kate and Ethel the big bed. Adeline sleeps on the cot, and Mary in the smaller crib with Mollie in her room; and Charles, Sr., sleeps alone in his glory in the spare room.

Mother herself, with the twins, occupied the room adjoining the tenement described in the first sentence of this quotation.

Congestion became somewhat less acute when the wet nurse and her baby finally departed, but not until Adeline at fourteen was graduated to a room of her own on the third floor did any member of the family, babies in their cribs excepted, ever have a bed to himself. Once out of the crib we slept double. A long bolster was put between pairs of children. It was intended to define clearly the half of the bed each child was to occupy, but instead of keeping the peace, it led to endless contention; a bolster fight was the regular prelude to sleep. The winner twined himself about the bolster, and the loser slept without the comforting warmth of feathers.

The fourth room on the second floor was what I suppose the English would call a day nursery. No one slept in it until many years later, when it became first Charles's room and then the guest room. During its first incarnation it was the center of the children's life. Its furniture consisted chiefly of two chests of drawers and a massive box couch of such incredible hardness that it would have bruised anyone who had tried to sleep on it. Its extraordinarily heavy lid opened upon a cavern in which the little girls' summer dresses lay stiffly starched—I suppose because there was no room for them in the painfully narrow closets in the bedrooms. Had the

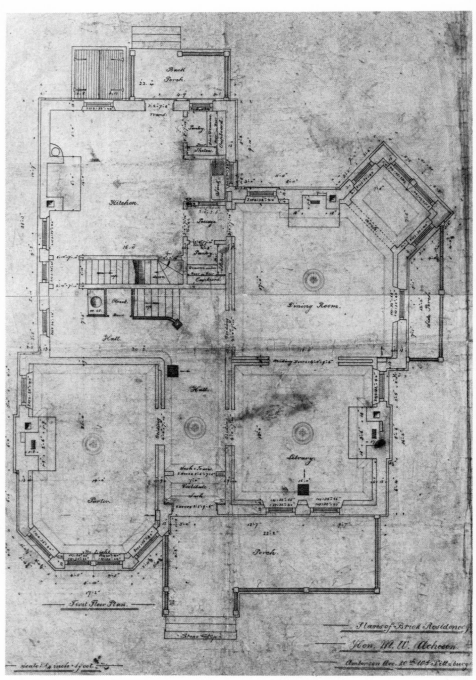

Floor plan of 719 Amberson Avenue. First floor.

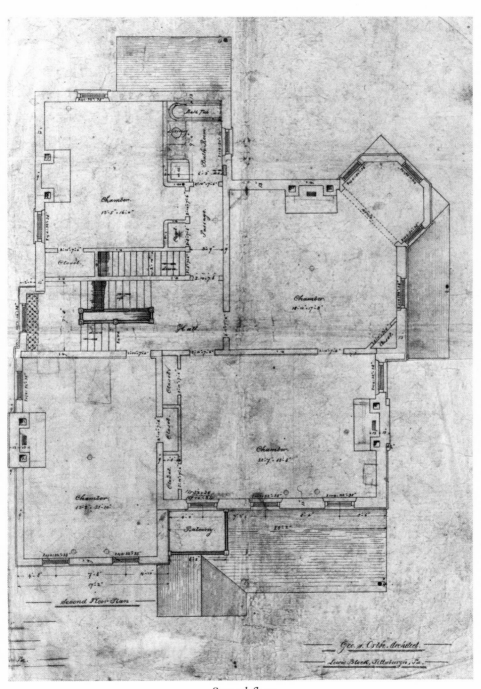

Second floor.

lid of this couch ever fallen on anyone's head, death would have been the instant result. But it was a wonderful piece of furniture for play; chairs placed upon the broad top transformed it into a train, a street car, a carriage, a sleigh—whatever the mood of the moment demanded. The larger chest of drawers contained sewing materials and household supplies, but the smaller one was ours. In it each of the five younger children had a drawer of his own, the sacred repository of his dearest treasures. (I do not know where our two older sisters kept their possessions.) The worst crime anyone could commit was to tamper with the drawer of a brother or sister, for the right of private property was rigidly enforced in our nursery. A nondescript rug covered the floor, its bumpy texture and brown and red coloring making it look, according to Betts, as though it had emerged from a meat grinder. Over the mantelpiece hung a large framed picture of the H. C. Frick coke works, and a picture of three big locomotives coming straight for us along diverging tracks adorned another wall. The chief distinction of the nursery was its closet, the only big one in the house. Built over the back stairs, it was large enough to hold even the chair that turned into a stepladder. Here our toys were kept in built-in drawers and on shelves that mounted like steps to the ceiling. It was a very desirable closet, and the nursery was an entirely satisfactory room, the only one in the house when we were young that was peculiarly our own. We *lived* there; the bedrooms were only for sleep.

The third floor was also in part our special preserve. Originally it contained only three rooms—one for the maids, one for storage, and one for play. The playroom which ran the whole length of the house, was enormous. The Amberson Avenue end of it belonged to our nurse, and when Mark was the next-to-the-youngest baby he slept in a crib beside her bed. The back half of the room was ours. At the southeast corner of our end a low door opened into a tiny gable room that was our playhouse. It had a sloping ceiling just high enough for children and a large casement window with pink and yellow squares of glass in it. During the infancy of the twins we temporarily lost both playhouse and playroom. So that two nurses might be accommodated, a partition was put up across the middle of the big room. Augusta, brought in to look after the twins, occupied what had been the playroom, and Mollie, the senior nurse, finally had a room of her own uncontaminated by children's toys. When Augusta was no longer needed, our playroom, though sadly curtailed, was restored to us. Later it became still smaller when closets for storage, with big drawers beneath them, were built all the way across one wall. It remained more or less a playroom, however, until even the youngest children ceased to need it, and then the trunks and boxes and pieces of discarded furniture that had long been encroaching took over and the playroom degenerated into a storeroom.

This encroachment probably began when the original storeroom in the northwest corner of the third floor was transformed by carpenter, paper hanger, Mother, and helpers into a room of incredible beauty for Adeline. The box seat built beneath the front windows with bookshelves at either end; the floor covered with matting and the walls with pink paper; the washstand table with a full petticoat of dotted swiss around it; the china washstand set on top of it and the gorgeous slop jar beside it, all adorned with roses that matched the wallpaper in color; the magnificent brass bed—such a masterpiece of interior decoration had never been seen in our house before. Years later when Adeline had married and her room had lost its glory Kate undertook its rehabilitation. With characteristic ambition she repapered it herself, banished washstand and washstand china, and covered the walls with pictures she had brought home from Europe. But it is the room that was Adeline's reward for achieving the ripe age of fourteen that made the most lasting impression upon me.

The rooms on the third floor opened off a square hall of considerable size. Its most important piece of furniture in the later years was a tall chest of drawers known as the mausoleum. During our childhood it stood in the bay window of the room adjoining Father and Mother's, an object of great interest to all the children because Father's pistol resided in the next-to-top drawer. Though we were allowed to look at it, we viewed its resting place with feelings of pleasurable terror. By the time Mary had finished college, however, the pistol had lost its fascination and she banished the mausoleum to the third floor. There it continued to be an object of interest because it was the repository of the family silver. Below the pistol drawer a broad panel let down until a chain inside stopped it at desk level, but the cavern within was never used as a desk; as long as I can remember it was the storage place for the silver. In our Victorian childhood solid silver, in our house at least, was not intended for daily use. We customarily ate with plated spoons and forks and cut our meat with black-handled knives while the real silver tarnished undisturbed in the mausoleum. Mother's solid-silver tea set, her silver knives and forks and spoons and butter plates emerged from seclusion only two or three times a year.

In summer when we went away Mother always hid these treasures in what she regarded as unlikely spots—knives between mattress and bed springs, forks in the blanket chest, butter knives in the camphor closet, spoons in the soup tureen of her wedding china, which moldered, unused like the silver, in the cupboards of the vast sideboard in the dining room. In later days when our silver was in daily use she always had difficulty in remembering where she had hidden it, and we would eat with kitchen cutlery until she had time to make an all-out search. Once she hid some treasures so effectively that we thought thieves must really have carried them off, but two or three years later during a thorough housecleaning of the storeroom they turned up in a drawer full of skates.

There was less romance and less concentrated living on the first floor of 719 than on the second and third floors. The house was square. To the right of its central hall as one entered was the library and to the left the parlor. The parlor went through many transformations and toward the end of our occupancy of the house it became a living room, but in our childhood no one could have lived in it happily. It was meant for occasions—for formal calls, for receptions, for Sundays, but not for everyday living. No one could have relaxed in its overstuffed rocking chair of vast proportions or felt at home with its tall china lamp, a Victorian monstrosity of the first order. In the glow of Christmas enthusiasm on December 26, 1895, Mother wrote thus of its charms:

He (Father) gave me the most beautiful and handsomest
lamp I have ever beheld—brass base, with vase-shaped bowl
I suppose it would be called, and large globe—green below
with bunches of beautiful pink and pale yellow roses and
chrysanthemums on both. Oh it is a beauty.

A large engraving in a broad and elaborate frame stood on an easel
in the corner between the sliding doors and the rosewood piano.
On either side of the piano hung oil paintings in gold frames that I
regarded as very beautiful, though quite unlike anything in nature
I myself had ever seen. At one time there was an engraving called
Wedded above the piano—a picture of a bearded gentleman with
an arm about a gently clinging lady, both gazing into space from
the top of a tower. Later it moved upstairs to adorn the walls of
Mary and Elizabeth's room, where I dare say it helped mold their
conception of wedded bliss. The artistic appearance of the parlor
was further enhanced by the rosy light that came through a
colored glass panel above the front windows. It shone through
heavy lace curtains that gave the crowning touch of formality to
the parlor. Though lace curtains stretching from ceiling to floor
hung at most of our windows, they had a look of austerity in the
parlor that they had nowhere else. Mother spent hours pinning
ten-foot long curtains to stretchers when they had to be washed—
which was about twice a month in those days of uncontrolled
smoke.

The library across the hall from the parlor was so called because
in one corner there were built-in bookcases with drawers below
them in which games were kept. Between the fireplace and the
front wall stood a combination bookcase and desk of golden oak.
In the pigeon holes of the desk Father stored cancelled cheques,
bound together in neat bundles by rubber bands at both ends.
Against the tremendous sliding doors between library and dining
room stood a couch on which Father often took forty winks under
a silky, dark blue cover with a many-colored border. Sometimes he
napped in the Morris chair that stood in the corner between
fireplace and couch. It was his special chair, but we all coveted it,

partly because it was the only comfortable chair in the room and partly because a book rest clamped to its side made it a highly desirable spot for reading. Beneath the couch Father kept a musical instrument, a zither I think, whose many strings we children loved to pluck. The most memorable piece of furniture, a game table, stood in the middle of the room. When one pressed a wooden disc at each corner of the underside, a drawer sprang out full of treasures—ivory chess men, poker chips of curious and varied shapes in enchanting little wooden boxes, cards, dominoes. In the center of the table a chessboard popped up when another disc was pressed. In the early years we were not allowed to use any of these treasures or even to press the secret springs very often, but merely to know that we owned such a magical table was joy enough.

On top of the mantelpiece stood a monstrosity that was Uncle George Reiter's wedding present to Mother—an ebony whatnot that reached to the ceiling. Its tall mirror was flanked by cabinets in which Father kept smoking supplies, and I think there was a shelf at the top edged with a miniature railing. Of the *objets d'art* that rested in the recesses of this horror I remember most vividly two pink-and-white china figures, a boy and a girl, each holding a basket in which were kept matches for lighting the gas. Between these two stood a big rectangular-shaped clock made of black wood and blue-and-white tiles that was a wedding present, I think from the Macbeths.

When winter came, heavy velour curtains were put up at the doors and windows of the library. They were hung in the dining room too, dark tan there and dull red in the library—lovely things for children to hide behind or twirl about in. The fact that there were no heavy curtains in the parlor indicates how little that room was used. The two rooms in which a large part of daily life took place had to have protection against drafts. The winter curtains when they were first put up made the familiar rooms vaguely mysterious. Outside noises were hushed by their heavy folds, and our own voices sounded strangely muffled. When I think of the winters of my childhood, they have the muffled sound and the camphory smell that came with the velour curtains.

The nursery, February 1899: Mark and Fluffy,
Charles, Elizabeth.

Playing streetcar in the nursery, June 1902:
Sophie Acheson, passenger; Charles, motorman;
Elizabeth, conductor.

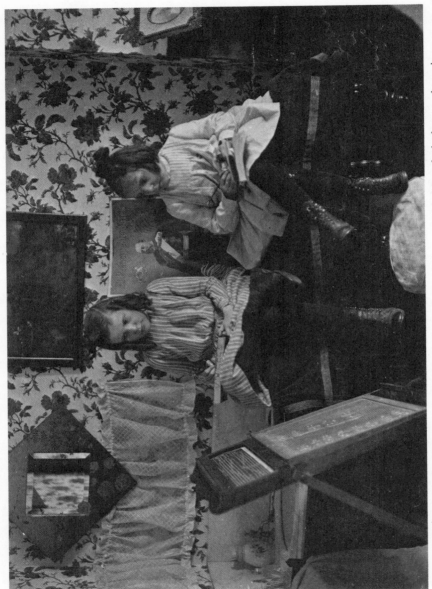

Mary and Elizabeth sitting on the organ in their room, February 1903. Note the built-in washstand.

Our parents' room, April 1899: Adeline on the couch with Mary and Mark; Elizabeth and Charles flanking the organ stool; Kate, with Fluffy, and Ethel reading. Kate's portrait is on the wall.

The parlor, October 1897.

Mark in the Morris chair in the library, April 1902.

Adeline in front of the parlor curtains, February 1905.

The dining room, May 1903.

Sunday lunch, May 1899: Elizabeth, Kate, Adeline, Charles, Mother, Mary, Ethel, Mark.

Father about 1900.

Ethel, March 1898.

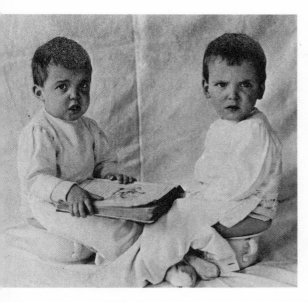

The twins, March 1898.

Mother reading to Mark, Ethel, Kate, and Mary while the twins shiver in their tin tub, 1897.

The seven Spencer children, June 1898.

Both library and parlor were lighted by gas chandeliers hanging from the center of the high ceilings. Each chandelier had about six gas jets, each protected and beautified by a glass shade shaped like a potty. To light the gas there was a long brown wooden pole with a wire guide attached, into which a long white wax taper fitted. First one lighted the taper with a match taken from the china girl or boy on the library mantel and scratched under the mantel shelf; then one turned the gas keys, one at a time, under each jet by means of a metal gadget at the end of the pole, and applied taper to gas. This was a laborious task when the gas merely spurted from a jet, but a nightmare when Welsbach burners in time came to supplant the jets. These burners, though they gave a much better light, were so fragile that they shattered at an unwary touch, and they were hard to light too. To put a new one on required patience and skill, and to keep it functioning required luck. In the library a gas bracket at either end of the mantelpiece supplied the light for reading, and these brackets being within reach of the hands were easier to manage than the chandeliers, but they were a trial too. No innovation ever brought greater relief to the inmates of 719 than the installation of electric light about 1919.

The chief distinction of the dining room was a big square bay window that jutted out from the southeast corner. In our early days it was occupied by an enormous wire plant stand on whose three or four tiers potted plants withered. No one in our house ever had a green thumb. In later years, after Father's retirement from business, his big rolltop desk turned the bay window into an office. On the wall between the bay window and the long window that opened on to a very narrow side porch stood a golden oak china closet, described by Mother in a letter written in 1893 as "Louis XIV, with a mirror at the back and glass front and glass concave sides." Beyond the long window there was another oak china closet, its triangular shape fitting neatly into the corner. On the shelves of these china closets the best glass and china rested undisturbed for most of the year. A walnut sideboard, later replaced by a massive one of golden oak, stood against the north wall. It was topped by a mirror with little cabinets high up on either side in which Father kept bottles and a tiny glass. We never knew what it was that he poured into the glass and drank before dinner; shielding our infant minds from evil, he called it tonic. A large assortment of high chairs and plain walnut chairs with cane seats stood against the walls, and a big table capable of indefinite expansion occupied the center of the room. When not in use it was covered with a heavy fringed cloth of dark colors. Above it hung the chandelier that the picture reveals more vividly than words can describe.

When we were very young an enormous bottle of spring water stood in the corner between the sideboard and the swinging door to the kitchen, for in those days typhoid fever raged in Pittsburgh, and city water was unfit to drink. Later, in order to cope with this problem, Father had a filter installed over the kitchen sink, and I can remember with fascinated disgust watching Mother every day clean tubes heavy with river slime. A pitcher of pure water always stood on a silver tray at one end of the sideboard ready for the thirsty.

All three downstairs rooms had doors that charmed generations of children. Between dining room and library the tremendous sliding doors were too heavy to be of any use to us, but the doors into the hall were the joy of every child that has ever entered the house. Light enough to slide open and shut with ease, they became, without the least effort of imagination, the doors of elevators. Three children at once could slide doors open and close them again with soul-satisfying crashes. The shutters in the three rooms gave almost as much pleasure. All the windows on first and second floors were shuttered, but those on the first floor were the most entertaining: three tiers, as against two upstairs, protected the long windows against marauders, and even the smallest fingers could open and close the lowest tier. The joy those shutters gave during the sixty-four years of Spencer occupancy of 719 is indescribable.

The kitchen, aside from a built-in speaking tube that connected it with the second and third floors, was unremarkable. Originally it had been equipped with a big coal range set into a recess in the chimney, but even during the first years it was rarely used. While 719 was being built, natural gas was discovered in Pittsburgh, and the house was made ready to receive it. When Mother and Father moved in on February 5, 1886, the coal range was already obsolete, and the ash pits in the cellar below the fireplaces were never used. From the beginning a gas cooking stove stood beside the range, and in later years the range was removed altogether to make room for a modern stove.

The only really remarkable thing about the kitchen of 719 was the food produced in it: steaks of incredible thickness and juiciness, for breakfast as well as for dinner in our early years; a whole school of jack salmon, crisp and succulent, on Sunday mornings; coffee ground in the kind of grinder one now pays a high price for in antique shops; ice cream made of real cream and ground in a tall tin can set in a wooden bucket and surrounded with ice and salt— how we loved to lick the dasher when it was removed! Of all the good food that came out of the kitchen, bread was the best. We baked twice a week, five or six big loaves at a time. Before the days of yeast cakes the children were sent to a house on the corner of Fifth Avenue and Lilac Street to fetch yeast, which we carried home in a small bucket. Bread making was a ritual. Something mysterious was done with yeast and flour at night, and then in a big tin bread bowl the mixture sat on the warm dining-room register all night wrapped in a red blanket. In the morning there were several kneadings and risings before the dough was put into pans for the final rise. When the pans went into the oven and the bread began to bake, the house was filled with a delectable fragrance. Only the taste of the crisp brown crusts themselves, thickly spread with good butter, was better than that lovely smell. There was a ritual too about the making of buckwheat cakes. They were also mixed at night, wrapped in the red blanket, and left on the register. Cooked for breakfast the next morning, those buckwheat cakes were like nothing that a generation brought up on packaged griddle cakes has ever tasted.

The only sad memory of the kitchen is of the disappointing emptiness of the sponge-cake bowl when Mother had finished scraping the last bit of the smooth pale-yellow mixture into the pan. No woman ever had greater mastery of the spatula! This uncanny skill in scraping a bowl so clean that it hardly needed to be washed her children were prone to forget, and when the moment came for licking they always felt cheated. But the cake itself was no disappointment; Mother's care in making it precluded failure. I can still see her weighing the eggs, changing a small egg for a larger one, taking one off the scales and putting another on until the measurement was exactly right; weighing the sugar and flour; squeezing the lemon juice and pouring it into the bowl; grating off some of the rind; tasting the batter critically and perhaps adding a little more lemon juice; whipping the whites of eggs until they were stiff and dry and then folding them gently into the yolks and sugar; and finally pouring the delectably smooth, pale yellow batter into the copper Turk's head pan that had belonged to her German great-grandfather. For some reason, Mother was inclined to leave in the mixing bowl more of every kind of batter than sponge cake batter. Perhaps the sponge cake bowls only *seemed* emptier than cookie and layer-cake bowls because sponge cake, even raw, was so good.

Looked back upon, Sunday lunches were disappointing too, though I don't remember resenting them particularly in my childhood. There were several reasons to account for their sparseness. In the first place, Sunday was Sunday and one did not work either oneself or one's maids unnecessarily. In the second place, Sunday dinner was at four o'clock in the afternoon, and therefore no one, it was thought, needed a cooked lunch. And so, when we came home from church, we gathered, sometimes in the kitchen and sometimes in the dining room, and lunched upon milk or lemonade and crackers. The children liked to break up oatmeal crackers in their milk and spoon up the unpleasant-looking mess. Not until they acquired spoons with thin tubes in them through which they could suck as through straws did they take their liquids straight. These were extraordinarily unhygienic spoons, but extraordinarily pleasant to drink through—at least until disillusionment set in. Even the most ardent sucker turned in time against a spoon too deeply encrusted with soap and ancient remains of cocoa. But when new, those spoons greatly enhanced Sunday lunches. In her later years Mother used to look back on those lunches with horror and accuse herself of having starved her children, but I think that the joy of mashing up oatmeal crackers in milk and sucking lemonade through unhygienic spoons compensated for whatever pangs of hunger we may have felt.

The food that was cooked in our kitchen came chiefly from four places: dry groceries from Stevenson's, meat from some independent butcher, vegetables and fruit from Page's, and butter, eggs, chicken, and vegetables in season from the country market in town. Stevenson's telephoned for our order every week, but the butcher got his by word of mouth daily. Howard, the driver for Eckert and Fry with whom Mother dealt for many years, would stand at the foot of the back stairs, and Mother, standing by the gate that kept her children from falling down the stairs, would tell him what to bring tomorrow: steaks, roast beefs, roasts of lamb, lamb chops—in those good old days meat was cheap and meat orders were generous.

Mother began to buy vegetables from Mr. Page early in her married life. When memory began for me, his shop was a wagon with a big bunch of bananas hanging at the end that came daily to our door. It was not long, however, before he had a store on Aiken Avenue near enough to be within easy reach. When something had been forgotten, one of the children was sent there to fetch it in a hurry. When the bill was to be paid, we clamored for the privilege of acting as messenger, for Mr. Page always gave us a present with the receipt. Once he gave me a whole box of apricots, and Betts remembers with pleasure boxes of Four O'clock Teas. Mother always said that everything one bought from Tom Page was good and that he gave good measure. She dealt with him until his prices rose so high that she could no longer afford to patronize him, but she left him with regret.

Our butter and chickens and eggs generally came from the Pittsburgh market, which Mother visited every Saturday morning till the last year of her life. The buying of butter was an art. I can still see Mother going about from country woman to country woman, eyeing their rolls of butter critically, taking up an end of the paper in which a roll was wrapped, nipping off with it a bit of butter, tasting it appraisingly with rapid smacking of the lips, and as a rule rejecting it. A country woman with a good pound of butter one week was just as likely as not to bring in a bad one the next week, so the tasting ritual had to be gone through with every Saturday. The buying of chickens was just as ritualistic, though here it was a question of the breast bone. If the end of that bone was still flexible, the chicken was young, but it had to be fat as well as youthful, and shapely. From the country market Mother brought home other treasures—the first garden peas of the season, delicious as peas have never been since they have been obtainable all the year round; boxes of shelled lima beans, tiny and succulent; fresh corn; delicious little squabs for a child recuperating from illness. In the spring she occasionally brought bunches of delicate hepaticas or trailing arbutus or trillium. The butcher usually brought her marketing home when he delivered the meat, but she often came staggering back with her arms full of good things.

The food that came from market and Page's and the butcher's was kept in the cellar under the dining room. Baskets of vegetables and fruit sat on a long bench against one wall, and the big double-doored ice box against the opposite wall held the more perishable things. Beyond a door beside the ice box other supplies were kept. A partition had been put up in that cellar during our childhood when crowding in the attic had become acute, with the intention of using the inner section as a storeroom. It was never so used, however, because it proved to be damp, and it promptly became a second food cellar. Bushels and bushels of potatoes were stored there, for we were oblivious to more recent dietary notions and happily ate potatoes every night for dinner. A barrel of apples always stood near the mountainous pile of potatoes, usually Northern Spies or Kings, which we were allowed to raid every day after school. No apples have ever tasted so good since as the crisp, tart, juicy apples from those barrels.

In the front food cellar there was a big closet in which preserved food was kept. On its shelves sat glasses of blackberry, grape, peach, black raspberry, and currant jelly and jars of peach butter, whole peaches, plums, and tomatoes. During the summer the children were called upon to help preserve these delicacies. We pulled grapes and currants from their stems, removed skins from tomatoes and peaches, and stirred peach butter endlessly with a

24

long wooden stirrer. These tasks were rather boring, but we all liked to see the shelves of the fruit closet full.

The two front cellar rooms were devoted not to food, but to heat. The room to the left of a central hall was the coal cellar. Father always bought a whole carload of coke at a time, which he and Grandfather divided between them. Our half filled the coal cellar to the ceiling. I can still see the man hired to put it there wheeling his barrow all day between the pile of coke that had been dumped on the street in front of the house to the little iron coal door at the side and still hear the bumping of the coke as it slid noisily down a metal trough into the house.

The furnace cellar was directly across from the coal cellar. It contained a furnace that was intended to heat only the first floor of the house and the coldest bedroom on the second floor, the one with a north and west exposure. Some years after the house was built Father had another flue put into his and Mother's bedroom, but it never succeeded in carrying any noticeable amount of heat. Since in all the bedrooms there were fireplaces, most of them with Taylor burners, the upstairs rooms were not entirely frigid, but the house was cold enough to require the whole family, adults as well as children, to go through the winter wearing "union suits" with sleeves reaching to the wrists and drawers reaching to the ankles. Each gas fireplace had screwed to the mantel shelf above it an enamel bowl, attached to the screwing device by three brass chains. These bowls, filled with water, were called air moisteners and were supposed to make more salubrious air still chilly in spite of the best efforts of fires and furnace. The furnace did all it could to heat us until January of 1928, when it died in a burst of coal gas that came near to asphyxiating Mother. Before she lost consciousness she managed to call the maids, who in a kitchen without furnace heat were outside the range of deadly fumes. Thanks to them and to George Macbeth, whom they called in, and to hastily opened windows, Mother escaped with only a scare. But the old furnace was doomed. The new one that replaced it had so voracious an appetite for hard coal that we finally put in a gas burner, and from there on, though the upstairs part of the house was no warmer, we ceased to be slaves to the furnace.

25

Beside the furnace was a mysterious little box of a room known as the cold-air chamber. It had a window in it with bars instead of glass across the opening, and queer little slits and doors connecting it with the furnace. We never very fully understood what it was for, but it was a wonderful place to hide in when we ranged through the house in games of hide and seek. It was also a refuge for those who had committed such criminal acts as throwing mud at the Macbeth's kitchen windows.

There was another mysterious little room under the cellar stairs. It was walled off from the main hallway at the end of the last century when Father had become an ardent photographer and needed a darkroom for developing his pictures. A little red glass window between it and the laundry increased the mystery of a room we were never allowed to enter. Here were developed the innumerable pictures Father took of his seven children. Though we were his most frequent sitters, I cannot say that we cooperated willingly. When we came home from church on a Sunday morning, we knew too well what awaited us. The twins plodding upstairs hand in hand were more than once heard to mutter, "We're not going to have our pitchers taken;" but the spider at the top of the stairs always caught the two little flies just the same, and all their sisters and their brother too. The sunniest bedroom would be ready and waiting for the picture taking—furniture pushed out of the way, background set up, camera ready on its tripod, and the dark cloth at hand for Father to throw over his head when he focused his pictures. To make his victims less reluctant, he thought up all sorts of devices: we were made to wear each other's coats and hats; we were made to assume strange postures. Nothing, however, really reconciled us to our fate. What we hated most was to be lined up in steps according to age; innumerable photographs of the seven Spencers—Adeline glowering at the top end of the line, the twins cross at the bottom, and the other four looking glum in between—attest the disagreeableness of the Spencer children.

I think that Father was more interested in the scientific than in the artistic side of photography. He liked to try new lenses, new developers, new paper for printing his pictures. At the beginning of his career as photographer, inexperience resulted in some appalling distortions; too often his offspring appeared as hump-backed little monsters. In time, however, he learned all the tricks and took beautiful pictures from the technical point of view. Sometimes they were artistic too, but more by accident than by intention. The interest for Father lay in achievement of perfect detail, and most of his fun he found in his darkroom in the cellar.

The darkroom was at the end of the cellar hall. Beside it, under the cellar stairs, was another tiny room containing a toilet for the maids. When I consider the conditions under which servants had to live in those days I wonder why anyone was willing to enter domestic service. Our maids had washstands in their rooms, with the customary basins, pitchers, and soap dishes on them and a slop jar on the floor beside; but there was no bathroom for them, and they had to fetch water from a housemaid's closet on the second floor. Their toilet was in a dark hole under the cellar stairs, and there was no bathtub for them anywhere. If they bathed at all, it must have been in the laundry tubs. There was nothing unusual about these arrangements; our house offered as much comfort to servants as most others. It was not until after Father's death that Mother had one of the third floor rooms divided and a bathroom put into one half of it for the maids.

The family arrangements for comfort and cleanliness were almost as inadequate, for there was only one bathroom for all of us. To ease congestion washstands with running water had been built into Mother's and Father's room and the room that adjoined it. Both were enclosed in wooden panelling stained red to match the woodwork in the two rooms. The panelling in our parents' room enclosed two little cupboards. In the smaller of them was the keyhole for turning on the gas in the fireplace; in the larger one the family medicines were kept—bottles of tiny camphor sugar pills that we were given when we had colds, a bottle of yellowish camphorated oil that was rubbed on our chests for the same purpose, calomel tablets, dear little boxes full of homeopathic pills—empty bottles and full bottles, all rather ominous and interesting to the young.

Everything in the bathroom was also enclosed in red-stained

wooden panelling—the washstand, the tin tub, the toilet, the walls halfway up. The toilet, with its big red-panelled tank near the ceiling, flushed by means of a spring; when one arose, the seat sprang up releasing a spring that set the water system in motion. Built in beside the seat was a box for holding toilet paper. Mother, who was thrift personified, kept it filled not only with legitimate packs of toilet paper, but with bits of tissue paper salvaged from old dress patterns. When her seven children were at loose ends and demanded something to do, she would set them down with some old patterns or torn sheets of tissue paper and a pair of blunt scissors to cut the paper into pieces of suitable size and shape for the toilet-paper box.

The fact that the whole family had to depend upon one bathroom made chamber pots an essential part of household equipment. Without them the children could not have been properly trained in good after-breakfast habits. They remained in use in the bedrooms until perhaps the second decade of this century when Theresa, an otherwise exemplary maid, gave them their death knell by refusing to have anything to do with them.

Considering the pressure of nine people upon one bathroom, it is small wonder that we grew up in the Saturday night bath tradition. It must have been a heroic ordeal for Mother and Mollie to get us all clean even once a week. Each child in turn was put into the red-panelled, tin-lined tub, scrubbed thoroughly, and then, wrapped in a canton-flannel cape, hurried to the nursery. There one at a time we stood in front of the fire while Mollie dried us, and giggled at our distorted images in the curved brass fender that fitted between gas burner and gray slate hearth. The current baby when tiny was bathed daily in a folding rubber tub that hung on a wooden framework. A bucket was used to fill it, and after the bath a hard black rubber cock was turned to permit the water to flow from the tub back into the bucket—an operation we found enthralling. When the baby outgrew this first tub, he was graduated to a portable tin tub, which, well filled with twins, Father's pictures have preserved superbly.

We took bathroom congestion as a matter of course until Adeline's wedding, when with a house full of guests competition became unbearable. The last guest had hardly departed when Father called in carpenter and plumber and had a bathroom built over the back porch, opening into the room that had once been the nursery. From then on the new bathroom was the men's and the old one the ladies'. It must have been at this time that the red-panelled toilet and tin tub were ripped out of the old bathroom and what was then modern plumbing substituted. In the early 1920s Kate and Aunt Lide, who at that time were occupying the two front rooms on the third floor, had a bathroom put in between their rooms. Though so small that one had to fold oneself up in the minute tub, it relieved congestion materially, and from then on there was bathroom comfort in the Spencer ménage.

Household Staff

To keep such a household as ours going a considerable staff was needed, and fortunately for us wages were so low that it was possible for Mother to have adequate help. During the early years of her married life a dollar and a half appears from her account book to have been the normal weekly wages for domestic service in our house at least. I think that throughout our childhood it never rose above five dollars. There were always a cook, a chambermaid, a nurse—two nurses when the twins were babies—and a laundress. I think that Mother began with Irish maids, but she was too unimaginative, practical, and truthful to like Irish blarney. Our maids were usually German or central European, fresh from the old country. Well trained servants were not eager to work in a house so full of children as ours and anyway they would have been too expensive. So Mother engaged newly arrived immigrants, trained them, taught them to speak English and make bread, and then sadly lost them to husbands eager to take over such jewels. As a child I could not understand why, when we had lost one maid and had advertised for another, Mother always asked us to stay out of the house when she was interviewing applicants. It never occurred to me that if the seven Spencer children accompanied by four or five friends, should go rampaging through the house, a promising candidate might decide not to come. After they came, some of them objected to our tearing through the halls on Saturday mornings when they were trying to sweep up the week's dust, but most of them put up with us surprisingly well.

Of all the maids who lived with us Mollie, our nurse, was the most memorable. The spring of 1893 Mother and Father had made plans to go to the World's Fair in Chicago, taking the two oldest children with them. Mark and I, the only others at that point, were to be left at home under the guardianship of Grandmother Acheson and our nurse Bertha Krinne. A month or so before the time of departure Bertha announced that she was going to be married and wished to leave at once. Mother, whose heart was set on the trip, was cast into the depths of woe, from which Father's promise to put an advertisement in the paper failed to raise her. But she must have been intended to go to the World's Fair, for Mollie Reagan answered the advertisement. The depression of 1893 had forced her into domestic service; socially she belonged several pegs above it. For the twelve years she lived with us she gave our parents perfect peace about their children. Mother and Father could have gone round the world with complete confidence that Mollie would take care of our health, our manners, our morals, and our physical safety. We all adored her. Mark, as a baby, would not eat unless she held the spoon, and the rest of us were equally devoted, if less petted on her. She had beautiful, very long chestnut hair, which on occasions she let us play with. We loved to braid it into dozens of pigtails, each with a ribbon at the end. I remember how furious she was one evening when the door bell rang and she had to answer it with her hair in as many pigtails as Topsy's. She bathed us; she helped the little ones dress; she took us for walks; she took us to kindergarten; she escorted us to dancing school; she darned the stockings and mended the clothes; she did, in fact, anything that needed to be done. Without her I do not see how Mother could have survived the childhood of her seven children.

Long after she had left us Mollie told me that Tillie Fritz, the chambermaid who most bitterly resented our games in the halls during Saturday sweepings, used to laugh at her for doing so much for the Spencer children. "They'll forget you," said Tillie, "the minute you leave them." But we never did; she remained important to us to the end. All her children felt the same way about her. When she left us she took care of John Ricketson, and he and his mother loved her as we did. Later she became matron of the nurses' home at the Homeopathic Hospital (now Shadyside Hospital) and there she died of cancer early in the 1930s. Her funeral service was at our house. I think it would have pleased her to know that we all felt she belonged there.

When the twins were little and there were four under five, one nurse was not enough, and the young, plump and foolish Augusta—probably dubbed Gucky by the children—was brought in to help Mollie. I think she stayed about three years, just long enough to let the twins get on their feet and permit the older children to become old enough to look after themselves. My most vivid recollection of her is of the sleigh ride she wangled for some of us. The butcher's boy, in those days when I am sure winters were colder and snowier than they are now, delivered meat by sleigh when weather permitted, and being one of Gucky's admirers, he one day picked her up with her small charges. This experience endeared her to us, temporarily at least, and has colored rather rosily my memory of one who was by no means a jewel.

All the maids lived in our house except the laundress, but since she practically lived in the laundry we were hardly aware of her departure at night. Since there were no labor-saving devices and since a family of nine, six of them female, used a great many clothes, activity in the laundry was almost continuous. I do not remember individually the laundresses of our childhood, but I think they were always Negroes. I do remember vividly the laundry itself, to the right of the cellar stairs as one went down—the round black iron stove full of red hot coals, the black flatirons, dozens of them, that sat heating on top of it; the big copper boiler for the clothes, the smell of soapsuds and beeswax.

The laundress who meant the most to us was Minnie, a colored woman of vast proportions, whom Soph with fine irony in later years dubbed Minnow. [Soph, the daughter of George and May Acheson, whose mother died when she was two, spent much of her childhood in the Spencer home. After her father's death in 1913, she resided with the Spencers.] Minnie presided in our laundry for twenty-five years, beginning about 1910. The washing machine and the electric iron arrived before her regime ended, but she never ceased to boil the clothes. Sheets, towels, table linen (we used damask tablecloths and napkins at all meals in those days, each napkin carefully rolled in its owner's silver napkin ring after the meal)—all these household linens boiled by Minnie, dried on a line out of doors, and ironed with loving care, were beautiful to behold. Our clothes, after a sojourn in the laundry, came back to us with the same fine finish. Ruffled petticoats of varying sizes, muslin drawers with tapes at the top to tie the bulky garments round the wearers' waists, bright colored cotton dresses, pinafores, white shirts after first flapping on the clothesline in the backyard returned to the laundry in a big wicker basket to be ironed by Minnie. I can still see her lifting an iron from the stove with a heavy pad (made by Mother out of many layers of old blanket cut in circles and covered and bound at the edges with thick blue denim or striped ticking); holding it to her cheek or spitting on it to test its heat; changing a heavy iron for a light one; smoothing it by rubbing it over beeswax wrapped in a bit of muslin. When everything was just right she would begin to smooth a garment with the sure, unhurried motions of an expert. There was time in those days to make an art of laundry work, and Minnie was an artist without peer.

Most of the cooks who presided in our kitchen have dropped almost completely from my memory, but a few were unforgettable. Probably it was early in the first decade of this century that an advertisement put in the newspaper by Father brought one of the most interesting of them, Amanda, to our back door. A big overgrown girl of sixteen, she was so fresh from the old country that she had to be accompanied by a child interpreter. Though she had no references, Mother, liking her substantial build and plaintive eyes, took her anyway and never for a moment regretted having done so.

The opening days of Amanda's career in our kitchen were fraught with difficulties, partly because of racial prejudice and partly because of her ignorance of English. The chambermaid of the moment, Bertha Tretow, a very competent blond Nordic from Hamburg, Germany, looked down her nose at brown-eyed Amanda, who came from the borderland between Germany and

Poland. In time Bertha came to regard Amanda as a friend, but in the beginning I am sure that she thought Mother had made a grave mistake. The problem of communication between Mother and her new cook soon ceased to exist, for Amanda learned quickly. In the early days she followed Mother about like a faithful dog, watching her every move. She would pick up each bowl and spoon the minute it ceased to be needed and say, "Washen dis, Missis?" Mother was never really daunted by the barrier of language; she could always get round it by a little dumb show. When, for instance, she wanted Amanda to fetch a chicken from the ice box she would point to the basement, flap her arms, and say "Cock-a-doodle-do," and Amanda would trot down to the cellar and return triumphantly with the chicken. It was not long before she learned enough English to make communication easy, and by that time she had broken down Nordic prejudice too, for she possessed every possible virtue.

From the beginning her chief ambition in life was to bring her mother to America. Her father was already in Pittsburgh, and between them they managed in time to save enough money for this purpose. They bought a ticket and sent it off triumphantly. Before it reached Germany, however, a letter came to Amanda from her sister. When she opened it, out dropped a piece of her mother's shroud. I can still see the look of grief in her brown eyes and hear her plaintive voice as she told us of her mother's death.

I do not remember how long Amanda lived with us—probably not more than two or three years. During that time she learned to make superb bread and in general to cook very well. Perhaps it was the summer of 1907 that she was to go away with us to Marion to cook for the Spencer-Curry-Acheson household, but instead we had to leave her in the hospital suffering from an attack of typhoid fever. Before we got home Mother received a letter from her, written we thought by Mr. Klein himself, for Amanda's English was not yet equal to such elegancy of style. In it she announced that she was going to marry Mr. Klein who had been "so good to me when I in hospital bed did lie," and she went on to thank Mother for all she had done for her, for which kindness Amanda hoped some day to be able to give thanks "in manners more substantial as by words."

From then on we heard of her only occasionally through Bertha Tretow. Once after an evening call Bertha reported with disgust that when Mr. Klein did not come home for supper Amanda put the steak back in the ice box and ate scraps. But this policy must have paid off for the Kleins prospered. Years later, perhaps in the early 1930s, Amanda came to our house one day to see Mother. Completely American in appearance and in excellent command of English, she was quite an impressive person, an example of the American success story at its best. One of her sons, she told us, was a doctor, and the other was studying mathematics at Carnegie Institute of Technology. I think Mother felt proud of having helped to make so worthy an American citizen as Amanda.

Nellie Pelz succeeded Amanda, if not immediately, then before many years. A Polish peasant, she had come directly from the fields of Poland to Pittsburgh, where before reaching our kitchen she had had the job of potato peeling in a restaurant. Whether it was the endless monotony of that work or her peasant background that made her so quiet we never knew, but she was the most silent and impassive person I have ever met. Though she was a pretty girl, madonnalike in appearance, her face was almost expressionless. And so was her voice. I never remember its slow, monotonous tone changing except when the sins of the coal range in the cottage we lived in for two summers in Edgartown stirred her to a mild kind of fury. "The biscuits would cook better on the sidewalk, Mrs. Spencer," she complained on one occasion. Occasionally a smile would lighten her face, but far more characteristic was a look of hopeless patience, a calm that must have been her heritage from generations of downtrodden peasants. She lived with us for a number of years, and when she left us to marry Mike Luczyk of Braddock we missed her. Though from external appearances she was completely emotionless, she must have been fond of Mother, for never a year passed that she didn't return to Amberson Avenue to call, bringing with her pictures of her children. It was hard to keep a conversation going, for having shown her pictures, Nellie would sink into an almost unbreakable silence. Prodded into speech by Mother, she would let fall bits of information that showed her to be active in good works. I think she came to occupy an important position in the Polish community of this district, but she never was one to volunteer information. Her visits continued till the very end of Mother's life. The final one came on the day of Mother's funeral, when Nellie appeared at the house in the morning to see whether she could help, and stayed through the service at the church to pay her last respects to a friend.

Anna Blattau belonged to a later day than Nellie. She and her sister Katherine practically stepped into our kitchen from the ship that brought them from Germany in 1925. Knowing not one word of English, they were so eager to learn that they were unwilling to go to the country with us that summer until I promised to set up a night school of my own to take the place of the night school they wished to go to in town. My best efforts, however, and the efforts later of night-school teachers in Pittsburgh, did not produce the results intended. Anna, after more than thirty years in America, still speaks nothing that can properly be called English. I do not mean that she cannot communicate, for she is fluency itself, and what she says is entirely understandable. But she is one who sweeps rules before her, with fine disregard of pronunciation, tense, inflections, and declensions she pours out a language of her own. When she is with me, I yearn for a tape recorder to take down her words as they fall from her lips, for her verb forms in particular are so improbable that I never can remember them. When in doubt she manufactures new words to suit her convenience. She once told me for instance, that something was "more exschpensier" than she wished to pay. A German niece who married a G.I. and came to America to live after the war won Anna's disapproving censure because of her highfalutin' ways. Shaking her head over Hildegarde's sins Anna said, "I think, Miss Ettel, she have too high schpleens in her head." German idiom translated literally into English also gave flavor to Anna's speech. When I started off to school in the morning she was all too likely to say, "Your petticoat looks out, Miss Ettel." And once when she was suffering from serious thyroid trouble she told me that her health was "going the hill down." Her language and delivery are so idiosyncratic and dramatic that I have always felt that the stage was deprived of a priceless comedian when Anna took to housework.

It is impossible to do justice to Anna on paper, but the story of her cousin's death perhaps suggests something of her flavor. She reported to us one day that her cousin had died and been given a magnificent funeral. "The coffin, Miss Ettel, it cost fifteen hundert dollar," and she smacked her lips over its beauty. Outraged by such extravagance, I protested that $1,500 was too much to pay for a coffin, but Anna was shocked that I should want to deny the cousin this compensation for spinsterhood. "I tink not so, Miss Ettel. My cousin she an old maid. She have nodding in dis life. I tink it right she have a gut funeral."

From the beginning Anna was determined to find herself a husband and settle down in America. Her first suitor was unfortunately a Protestant and the courtship dragged while she tried to persuade herself that marriage with him would not cause her soul's damnation. Her philosophizings on this score were always superbly practical. "If I go marry Shojn," she would say, "we marry not in de schurch. Dis is gut, I tink. If we like it not, we get divorced." Fear of public opinion, however, caused her to hesitate. "My friends they say we not married; we live yust like cats and dogs." Pamphlets sent by Papa Blattau describing her future in hell if she persisted in her wicked intention of marrying John finally put an end to this romance and opened the way for a second suitor. Charlie Gilchrist, Scotch Irish, Protestant and about fifteen years older than Anna, finally won the prize by changing his religion to match hers. I do not believe he has been a very good Catholic, but Anna has told me over and over again that "Sharlie is a gut man; he make me a gut husband."

The marriage did not take place until Anna had lived with us for eight years, during which time she had become a magnificent cook, quite indispensable to Spencer comfort. All our maids respected Mother, and many of them loved her. If the work at 719 was hard, as it undoubtedly was, it was work done for one who was always reasonable, fair, and considerate. Thanks to Mother herself being what she was, she was well served through the years and had the help she needed to cope with her big family.

"Up to Her Ears in Sewing"

One household activity Mother took largely upon herself: the manufacture of clothes. Though the great spurts of effort came in spring and autumn, dressmaking really went on in our house fairly constantly throughout the year. With herself and five daughters to clothe, Mother never caught up with the needs of her family, and since she had neither a natural liking for sewing nor a flair for designing, she had to struggle with an occupation that went against the grain. Necessity forced her, however, at least twice a year to take stock of our garments in order to insure our being suitably clothed for the oncoming season. Once, I remember, when a period of illness and quarantine had prevented this yearly survey she was horrified over the clash of colors when we started out for church one Sunday and had to seat us with great care in the pew so that orange, red, and cerise were separated. "I keep well, thank God; and am busy as ever—must get Mary's winter clothes finished or she will be bedridden for want of decent covering!" Mother said in a letter to me dated November 20, 1906, a comment that indicates the difficulty she experienced in keeping up with her job.

Fortunately for her the number of clothes each daughter in common decency required was small, though even one set of small requirements multiplied by five made a formidable total. We each had in winter one good dress, one school dress, and one play dress (cotton dresses for hot weather had to be more plentiful); one pair of good shoes, one pair of school shoes, and one pair of play shoes; a good hat and school hat; and for Mother and the older daughters one handbag to go with everything. There was no such nonsense as matching accessories. Certain things not often needed we shared. Mother's Roman sash, for instance, that she herself had worn as a girl she lent to each daughter as it was needed. Every one of us in turn encircled her waist with the gay stripes of that sash and enjoyed the distinction it gave. It was made of good stuff, for

Lunch in the nursery, April 1898: Elizabeth, Gucky, Charles.

Amanda, April 1906.

Mollie and Elizabeth, March 1900.

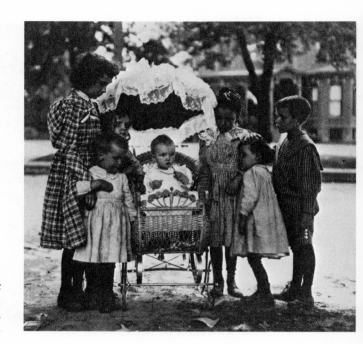

Summer clothes, 1899: Kate, Charles, Mary, Sophie Acheson, Ethel, Elizabeth, Mark.

Fashions in underwear, June 1901: Ethel, Sophie Acheson, Charles, Elizabeth, Mark.

Fashions in outerwear, March 1901: Charles, Elizabeth, Mary wearing Ethel's red coat, Wilbur Spencer, Mark, Elizabeth Crabbe.

The twins in their best winter clothes, January 1898.

Ethel and Kate in their homemade hats, May 1903. Ethel is wearing the Roman sash.

Ethel in the Spanish dress, July 1898.

Ethel in a stylish suit, April 1906.

even today after an existence of perhaps ninety years it still could be tied around another young waist were need to arise. We also borrowed Mother's single pair of black silk stockings when as teenagers we went to parties. They were of such heavy texture that not a trace of skin could possibly show through, but to us in our youth they seemed the final touch of elegance. The ostrich feathers that enriched our hats were similarly shared. In a letter written to me at boarding school October 26, 1906, Mother tells me to "let Kate bring your Leghorn hat home for the sake of the feather which she *may* need." There was still in the camphor closet when we emptied 719 in 1950 a big box of tired-looking ostrich plumes hoarded against possible need.

By thus sharing her treasures Mother kept down the number of purchases, but even so clothes were a never-ending problem, partly because they cost more than she had to spend and partly because hardly anything could be bought ready-made. When things *had* to be bought, the purchases were staggered. Never, for instance, until 1902 when Uncle Mark's wedding forced such extravagance did we all have new shoes at once. What was bought we had to take care of and make last. When we came home from school we changed into play clothes; when church and Sunday School were over we took off our Sunday finery. If through carelessness anything was destroyed we had to repair or replace it. When Fluffy was a puppy he chewed up so many things that the edict went forth that each of us must be responsible for any damage he did to possessions we had carelessly left about. One Saturday morning when Kate and I were to go to town with Mother, Kate could not be found. Mother gave me carfare, told me to find Kate and follow her. When she had gone I found poor Katie sobbing in a playhouse we had made out of dust sheets in Mary's and Elizabeth's room. In her hands was one of her best shoes, its bottom buttonhole chewed off by Fluffy. With my tears flowing in sympathy we rode to town to meet Mother and tell her of this ghastly tragedy. True to her word she made Kate pay for the damage, but she tempered the wind to her poor little shorn lamb: she had the shoemaker patch the shoe for a quarter instead of requiring Katie to buy a new pair. By such methods she taught us so well to take care of our clothes that I change from good clothes to less good as soon as I get home from a party.

When it became absolutely necessary, new clothes were supplied, but since no decent ready-made garments were available for girls, to get hold of what we needed was not easy. Even some of our underwear had to be made at home, and in consequence Mother spent much of her life at the sewing machine. There were night garments to make for the twins, with long legs and enclosed feet to keep them warm all over. After days of cutting out, stitching at the machine, making buttonholes by hand, sewing on buttons, I remember her disgust when four little nighties were finished and there were after all that toil only two apiece for her babies. There were flannel petticoats to make too: dark gray flannel attached to a white bodice for school, white flannel, feather-stitched, for occasions. White cotton petticoats went over the flannel, and these were trimmed with Swiss embroidery or lace-edged ruffles. I remember Mother toiling over petticoats for Adeline's trousseau, especially over the one for the wedding. With its rows and rows of fine tucks, lace insertion between and a lace edge at the bottom, it was a genuine labor of love. There were corset covers too, lace adorned, with eyelet insertion at the top through which to run baby ribbon. Our basic winter garment, the union suit that covered us snugly from wrists to ankles, and the Swiss knitted cotton shirts we wore in the summer came from the store, and so did the heavy muslin drawers on draw strings that Mother and the older girls wore, and the panties and "panty body waists" of the younger children, and the boneless Ferris waists we graduated to in adolescence, and of course the heavily boned, tightly laced corsets of the grown-ups. But the next layer of covering, between underpinnings and dresses, was produced on our sewing machine, with sometimes a little hand embroidery added to give class. Even suits for the little boys were custom made, but fortunately not in our house. Mrs. Landrum manufactured their clothes in her own home until Mark and Charles were old enough to wear woollen suits. These could be bought at department stores long before attractive dresses were available for girls.

The undergarments Mother could make herself, but dresses

required professional help. Every spring and every autumn, and often in between times, a seamstress arrived to get us ready for the coming season or for some special occasion. To find a good one was another recurring problem. The letters Mother wrote me when I was at boarding school are full of such passages as these:

> We seem to be fated about seamstresses! The one I had for three days before Thanksgiving and who was certainly not worth the $1.75 she asked per day, has been very sick & unable to return. And "Zatella" is also ill and writes for me not to depend upon her. (December 11, 1906)

> Your poor sister Mary is still wearing summer dresses because I cannot get competent people to help me finish the garment begun long ago. (December 2, 1906)

> Lizzie, Aunt Ethel's seamstress, disappointed me, but since Wednesday have had the Dempsey girl you and I tried to find on Kelly St. last summer. She is slow, but painstaking and careful. (January 11, 1907)

Evidently the Dempsey girl proved a feeble reed, for on April 27, 1907 Mother wrote:

> I have a pink gingham ready to finish for you after you have tried it on. Katherine Dempsey grew so befuddled over it that I had to take it from her at last, and will now leave it until I see you.

If the seamstress were any good, she supplied ideas, cut out the materials Mother had provided, put together the pieces, and fitted the lucky owner. Mother took out bastings, made buttonholes, sewed on buttons and hooks and eyes, whipped seams, and put the final finish on the garment.

Clothes were so constantly on Mother's mind that they even followed her to bed and haunted her in her sleep. "I had such a funny dream last night," she wrote me August 25, 1911, "shortly after your departure. First I thought Miss Inglis called up to tell us that she had reduced her prices temporarily; and though most reluctant, I ordered a dress for myself and one for one of you girls. Then in a night or two I dreamed that my gown came home. It was made of black cotton net—similar to the white we use for lining yokes—and was trimmed from bust to hips all around with *cards* of cheap sort of *china* buttons. Some of the cards being bright blue in color, and some red! Miss Inglis evidently saw disappointment in my face so she hurried to say that she had done this in order to add a 'touch of color' to the dress."

It goes without saying that where clothes were so hard to come by they were made to last forever. Of course we all wore hand-me-downs. A dress that began with Adeline, traveled down to Kate, then to me, to Mary, to Elizabeth, provided it was made of stout enough material to hold out until it reached the youngest. The most notable garment in this progression was a red coat that started with me in 1894 when I was a small girl. Made of the very best wool, it was intended to endure, and it did. Originally it had three little shoulder capes of which I was very proud. When in time I grew too tall for my coat, one cape was removed and turned into a yoke on which the body of the coat was hung and thus lengthened. After I had again outgrown it, the yoke was removed, and the coat thus shortened but now with only two capes became Mary's. For her it was in time lengthened, and she too wore it until she outgrew it. Then the whole process was repeated for Elizabeth. Year after year after year that coat walked all winter long to the Osceola School. It must have been missed there when even our youngest had finally to abandon it.

The Spanish dress too had a long, but dishonorable career. It was made for me while the Spanish war was in progress—a red and yellow gingham, the colors of Spain. How my patriotic soul hated that dress! My schoolmates teased me every time I wore it, called me Spanish, implied that I was a traitor; but I had to wear it anyway. And when I thankfully outgrew it, it passed to Mary and then to Elizabeth carrying with it a heavy load of built-in hatred. I don't think my little sisters had the faintest idea why it was hateful, but they loyally hated it anyway.

It was obviously advantageous both for Mother and for us that we should all learn to sew early so that we could help with the never-ending task of clothes making. I can hardly remember when I couldn't sew. By the time I was ten I was making handkerchiefs with rolled edges on which lace was neatly sewed. The year that Mary had diphtheria I had made some for my Sunday school teacher, Miss Emma McClintock, that had to be boiled before they could be presented, in order to kill any lurking germs. At eleven I made all the decoration for a white lawn dress; rolled lace-edged ruffles and a yoke of lace and insertion. My two older sisters were equally adept with the needle, and by sewing ourselves as we grew older we were able to enlarge our limited wardrobes.

Mother must have been relieved when her daughters took over any part of the dressmaking, for to her it was an uncongenial occupation. In rereading the letters she wrote me from 1906 through 1912 I was impressed by a number of things: how demanding I was, how thrifty she was, how constantly she toiled to satisfy us, how little time she had to bother with her own clothes. These extracts from her letters suggest far more than my words can:

> The seamstress question is uncertain. The suit I fully intended to purchase for thee; so set thy fears at rest. Kate suggests your both getting them when she is East, but you can wait until you come home if you so desire. Can you not use last year's one for "scuff"? (February 26, 1907)

> Did I write to you last Sunday? A guilty feeling has oppressed me all week as I sewed (have been doing scarcely anything else in my desire to leave my family at least reasonably well off for clothing when I leave them) that I had neglected you. (April 25, 1907)

Even on her holidays Mother remained "up to her ears in sewing," as Father aptly reported in 1894.

Relatives

The Achesons

The maids who lived with us when we were young were important because they kept the machinery of life going, though as the sewing burdens illustrate, they were only part of the household routine. Actually we took the maids for granted and never thought much about them until some cataclysm brought one regime to an end and started another. Much more important than these people who came and went, were the relatives who were a permanent part of life even though some of them lived too far away to be seen very often. The Achesons, because they were the most accessible, were the closest to us. Up the street, across from the church stood Grandfather Acheson's house, our second home.

Of the people who lived in it during our youth Grandmother Acheson has the least reality. She died a few months before our twins were born, and so even to the three oldest Spencers she is only a shadowy memory. I remember her vaguely as an old lady in a bonnet being pushed up the street in a wheelchair by John Organ. Only fifty-four when she died, she was actually never an old lady, but years of illness, together with the bonnet, I dare say created the illusion of age. Much more vividly than my grandmother I remember what we three eldest children wore when we were taken to see her for the last time. I can still see us in little red plaid dresses sitting on the top step of our front porch waiting to go to Grandfather's house, but how my grandmother looked in death I do not remember. By the time memory really begins, Aunt Ethel was in charge of Grandfather's house and Uncle Mark, not yet married, was still living at home.

We were in and out of that house constantly, particularly during the frequent incursions of the Gordons from Brookville, Pennsylvania. Aunt Kate Gordon, Mother's next younger sister, has told me that during the first year of her marriage she came home to her parents eleven times. When homesickness overcame her she would turn the pictures of her family to the wall, and then her kind husband would say, "Katie, I think you had better go home for a visit." By the time the Spencer children were old enough to remember she had overcome the homesickness, but she was in Pittsburgh frequently during our childhood. And always it seems to me as I look back on those visits, she went home with one more child than she had had when she came. Had I been a more sophisticated little girl, I should have known that the lumps of magnesia that Aunt Kate was always nibbling for heartburn were a sure sign of a baby in the offing; but I never learned to read the signs, and each new little Gordon caught me by surprise. I dare say she visited her parents at other times, but she always came to their house to have her babies—all five of them. I have vivid memories of the guest room, with its big four-poster mahogany bed and heavy wardrobe, overflowing with Gordons, a new baby lying in the white wooden cradle that had once rocked Aunt Kate herself and her brothers and sisters.

Since there was a Gordon to match almost every Spencer, life was eventful during those visits. Our favorite playground was the Reese property that adjoined Grandfather's. The Reese house was for many years unoccupied, and the stable behind it was empty, but to us both were inhabited. We could climb to the top of a shed that leaned against the stable wall and from this vantage point peer through the windows, hoping, yet fearing, to see the fiery-eyed monster with which Gordon imagination had endowed the stable. If a sharp eye detected the monster in some dark corner, we scrambled to the ground and ran screaming through the monstrously tall grass of the field that stretched all the way to Castleman Street. It still surprises me that tall grass today is so short; when I knew it best, it reached to my shoulders.

With or without the Gordons, Grandfather's house was a joy. The back hall, long and narrow, had wooden cupboards built in along one side. These ordinarily held brooms, cleaning equipment, and the like, but frequently they held children as well, either hiding or playing house. One of the front rooms in the attic contained the toys of Mother's brothers and sisters ranged on low shelves—wonderful treasures to explore in odd moments. In another storeroom an uncle's collection of birds' eggs always enchanted me. The bathroom on the second floor was another place of great interest because of the chart that hung on the wall. On it were pictures of Bible characters and verses from the Bible, a new picture and text for every month—perhaps every week—of the year. Next to the bathroom was the sewing room that Uncle George later turned into what seemed to us a super de luxe bathroom for his own private use.

The most interesting room in the house was Grandfather's study, which opened off the dining room. Shelves of law books reached to the ceiling. To get at them one had to mount a neat little sliding ladder, which always stood ready against one of the shelves—and how we loved to mount it. Grandfather's big table desk occupied the center of the room, and beside it stood a smaller table with a drawer in it in which he kept scraps of foolscap paper that were of great value to his grandchildren, particularly in conjunction with the pencils and the pot of mucilage that stood on top. Beside the smaller table there was a revolving bookcase that twirled around in a way that enchanted the young. In a corner near the door into the dining room a small round wash basin offered cleanliness not only to Grandfather, but to everyone else who needed a downstairs wash. The clean amber-colored cake of Pear's soap that lay ready for dirty hands was so pleasantly smooth and so unlike the common Castile soap we used at home that even the most reluctant washer rather enjoyed a good scrub.

Grandfather, though I never remember his speaking a harsh word to any of us, was a rather awe-inspiring person. The fact that he saved bits of foolscap for us and let us mess about with his mucilage suggests understanding of the young, but he seemed rather remote. And the twinkle in his eye sometimes baffled us by its suggestion of a joke we could not share. Once when the three eldest Spencers on an extended visit were participating in a Sunday evening Bible reading, giggles overcame them. I can still see him looking at us tolerantly over the top of his spectacles, waiting for the gigglers to regain control of themselves so that the reading could continue. It was during the same visit, I think, when I was spluttering about something with characteristic fury and demanding my rights that he began to address me as John Doe. I didn't understand why he called me by this name and from the twinkle in his very blue eyes, I knew he was laughing at me, but somehow his amusement never hurt my usually tender feelings. We were all fond of him, but from a distance.

Aunt Ethel, for whom I was named, kept house for Grandfather. Never a very independent person, she was constantly coming down the street to our house to consult with Mother. What she wished to talk about was probably the new maid or the cost of eggs or how much calomel to take, but she made such a secret of her mission that we were consumed with curiosity. She would draw Mother into a room, close the door, and carry on what seemed to us endless and mysterious conversations. Twice a year she accompanied Grandfather to Philadelphia where he held court. At the old Colonnade Hotel where they stayed on these occasions they came to be well known. One year when they appeared in the dining room for the first time the head waiter ingratiatingly whispered to Grandfather, "Judge your daughter is falling into fat." Adeline on hearing this remark promptly dubbed Aunt Ethel "Chubby," and Chubby she remained to her Spencer nieces and nephews to the end.

During the early years I remember Uncle Mark chiefly as an inciter to merriment. He disrupted the Sunday Bible reading once by calling Melchizedek "Milk-easy-dick"—a sally of wit that reduced his little nieces to helpless laughter. His marriage in 1902 I remember better than I remember him in his bachelor days. It was made memorable by the fact that all seven Spencers for the first time in their history had new shoes at one and the same time, and by Aunt Mamie's arrival carefully wrapped in a sheet to keep her white dress clean during the drive from Edgewood. After his marriage his bride endeared herself to us by letting us help her unpack wedding presents in Uncle George's house, which she and Uncle Mark occupied for the first years of their married life. Once she invited the Spencer children to a New Year's dinner and served as the *pièce de résistance* a baby pig, with an apple in its mouth. This was a culinary experience the like of which they had never before enjoyed, and it made an indelible impression.

The Reiters

Because Grandfather lived on Amberson Avenue, we knew his family more intimately than any of our other relatives, but no farther away than Edgewood, Grandmother Acheson's sisters, Great-aunt Mamie and Great-aunt Lide Reiter lived in the old house that had belonged to their father.

Aunt Lide, the youngest of the Reiter family, very early had her life blighted. At nineteen, though his own mother begged her not to, she married an entirely worthless man of great charm. Six weeks of marriage was enough to show her the full extent of her mistake, yet in spite of his drinking and carrying on with women I think she always loved John Black. About three years later, diseased and unhappy, she became pregnant, and then Victorian prudery and inadequate doctoring took their hand in ruining her life. When the baby was several weeks overdue, she approached her mother, only to be told that such things should not be discussed. Though her father was a doctor, it was still less proper for her to talk to him about so vital a matter. When the baby, with a tumor at the base of his head, was born at last to live for only a few days, Aunt Lide was horribly torn. The steps that were taken to help her were unavailing, and she went through life with the damage unrepaired. Spartan courage enabled her to endure her ills without ever a word of complaint, but she must have suffered physically all her life. By the time her baby was born her marriage was past saving, and her autocratic father insisted upon her getting a divorce, resuming her maiden name, and coming home to live.

Toward the end of the century Aunt Lide married Major Wolfe, veteran of the Civil War and lighthouse keeper at Sea Girt, New Jersey, and went to live with him first in the lighthouse and after his retirement in a cottage she built nearby. The second marriage was no more successful than the first. Major Wolfe was not her equal either intellectually or socially, and I think he drank. Since his sins were never referred to in our presence, I have always been a little vague about what they were. Anyway, Aunt Lide put up with him until Uncle Maje, as we children called him, retired in his old age to a home run by some fraternal order to which he belonged. He and Aunt Lide corresponded diligently after that by postcard, each card faithfully recording what each had eaten since last writing.

In our youth all we were aware of was Aunt Lide's queerness; the tragedy of her life we came only gradually to realize. Photographs show her to have been a beautiful girl with a crown of dark hair. The face of the woman we knew was ravaged by time and suffering, and her hair had become so thin that it hardly covered her scalp. Not even time, however, could bend her straight back or destroy her pride. Embittered by her experience with life, her health shattered, her hearing gone, Aunt Lide was not a happy person. The wrongs she had suffered in the past were ever with her. Many is the time she has told us with still lively bitterness of a man who promised her a lamb when she was a little girl but who failed to keep his promise. Although she never spoke to any of us of her unhappy marriages, she undoubtedly brooded over them in the same way as she brooded over the lamb, and deafness intensified her introversion.

During our childhood Aunt Lide came back to Edgewood at intervals for visits, but she did not return to stay until Aunt Mamie's death. Then she sold both the house in Sea Girt and the Edgewood cottage and boarded with a friend in Edgewood for awhile. After two or three lonely years there, she came at Mother's invitation to live with us at 719, and from then, October 1919, until her death in October 1925, she was a member of our family. At first she occupied the room on the third floor that had been Mollie's, but when she began to find stairs hard to climb she came down to my room at the head of the front stairs and I moved up to hers. During the first year or two that she was with us she refused to go to the country in the summer and insisted on staying alone in town, but this problem was solved when she gave Kate money to build a wing to the Coraopolis cottage. There in a room of her own she gathered her pitifully few possessions about her and I think really enjoyed life, with Kate established in a tiny room beside her.

During the six years she spent with us certain of her habits and ways of speaking and writing became part of our family tradition. In a city still notably dirty Aunt Lide's hands were incredibly clean; she was constantly washing them. The touch of those spotless hands, always cold, the skin smooth and dry with age, made one jump. She seldom sat for more than a minute at a time without taking her tatting out of a little bag and making her shuttle fly. This action was usually accompanied by the words, "I'm no needlewoman." She was however, a notable tatter. I wonder how many yards of tatting she made in the course of her seventy-seven years. She frequently presented us with neat little packets of it wrapped in tissue paper and tied with thread. Some of it was so fine and pretty that we could use it with pleasure, but too often it was coarse, with no virtue except that it was beautifully made, and we had difficulty in disposing of it. But fine or coarse, pretty or ugly, its manufacture continued as long as there was life in the cold clean hands.

Until she came to live with us her visits were brief. In no time at all after her arrival, her tatting would go back into its bag, and its owner remarking, "I'm no stayer," would slip away so silently that one was hardly aware of her going. Nothing irritated her more than people who, having announced their intention of leaving, lingered on at the door. Cousin George Cook Reiter's wife was one of these slow departers. A gregarious Southerner, she liked to talk, and there always was a long interval between the announcement of intention and actual departure. At the first indication that Helen and George were about to leave Aunt Lide would rise to her feet and begin to edge them toward the door. As Helen's chatter continued, Aunt Lide's expression became more and more disapproving. Finally when she could bear the delay no longer she would say dourly, "When you say you're going, go." She was glad to see them, but she felt about them as she felt about all visitors, that their calls should be short and promptly ended.

Unquestionably the years she spent with us were the happiest of her mature life. She called our house "The pilgrim's retreat," and she found in it the peace and affection she had always craved. She loved Mother; from the beginning she had found her so congenial a niece that she had very early given her a pet name, "Biddie." Once during her last years she said to her, "Mary, when I call you Biddie it means something," and she often called her Biddie. In the light of this remark it is touching to see the "Biddie" engraved on the backs of the gold-bowled silver coffee spoons she had long years before given Mother for a wedding present. Aunt Lide was very fond of Charles too, but Kate was undoubtedly her favorite. And no wonder—Kate has the understanding of human nature and the compassion that make companionship possible between old and young. Aunt Lide by the time we knew her was, I think, afraid of affection. When she came to see us in the days before she lived with us she would ward off kisses with a gesture of the hand suggestive of the archangel at the gates of Paradise warding off intruders. "C.Y.K. [consider yourself kissed]," she would say, and after a brief call she would depart, again unkissed. But once she had become a member of our family, she could not escape our company or our kisses so easily. Kate ignored both the warning hand and the injunction. She made a point of giving Aunt Lide both a morning and a good-night kiss. She made much of her, joked with her, gave her presents and time and affection, and the little aunt mellowed under this treatment.

Both the great aunts were in all things honest and direct, partly because of their upbringing and partly because of the practicality and unimaginativeness that were, we always thought, part of their north German heritage. They prided themselves on speaking the truth even when they might better have been silent. One of us, for instance, would appear in her best clothes ready to go out, feeling very elegant, and Aunt Mamie would prick the bubble of self-satisfaction with "You look like the devil in that hat." Nor did they confine their truth telling to the family. Aunt Lide, a woman of perfect integrity herself, expected others to follow the straight and narrow path of righteousness too, even in small matters, and pointed out their sins to them when they did not. Men who smoked and spat in streetcars in spite of signs requesting them to refrain had their attention called to the signs in no uncertain terms. Once riding in a crowded car with Kate she had to stand while a fat young man lolled in the seat in front of her taking up far more space than he was entitled to. Aunt Lide remarked loudly and pointedly to Kate, "All the pigs are not in the pen." This outspokenness Uncle George Reiter shared with his sisters. When I was about thirty, very well aware that my first youth was gone, he caught me one day as I returned home from a hard day's work, looked me up and down, and remarked, "Umph, you're beginning to show your age." Reiter frankness was not endearing, but the two great aunts at least spoke the truth on principle; truth was truth and must be spoken no matter how unpleasant. I am not sure that with their brother it was so much a matter of righteousness as of complete lack of concern for the feelings of other people.

During the summer of 1907, when we had a cottage at Marion, Massachusetts, he did the one thing for us that some of the Spencers remember with active pleasure. That summer he was cruising along the New England coast on a lighthouse tender inspecting lighthouses—probably his last assignment before retirement. One day his tender dropped anchor in the Marion Harbor, and a small boat, launched from its side chugged up to our float to fetch a contingent of Spencers—Mother, Charles, Elizabeth, probably Mary and me. We climbed aboard the launch, were ferried out to the tender, and taken on a cruise along the Massachusetts coast as far as the Gay Head light on Martha's Vineyard. At seventeen I was too old to get the thrill from this expedition that it would have given me earlier, but Charles at twelve found it one of the high points of his childhood. Near New Bedford we anchored off Ricketson Point and in the ship's boat landed and called on the Ricketsons and Scaifes, and then took some of them aboard with us for a brief cruise in Buzzard's Bay. To these guests, as to all non-relatives, Uncle George showed a suave courtesy that was never apparent in his treatment of relatives. Outsiders always thought he was wonderful.

Though we were properly grateful to him for letting us share his lighthouse inspecting, we could not regard him with admiration.

Grandfather's house, 832 Amberson Avenue.

Grandfather in his judge's robe, September 1905.

Aunt Ethel Acheson, about 1899.   *Uncle Mark Acheson, 1900.*

The family at Sea Girt, New Jersey, August 1900: back row, *Adeline, Aunt Mamie;* middle row, *Kate, Aunt Lide, Charles, Elizabeth, Mother;* bottom row, *Mark, Mary, Uncle Maje, Ethel.*

Lettice Adams.

Even as children we found him trying, and as both he and we grew older we found him increasingly unlovable. He had an eye for women, especially for beautiful women. The Spencer girls hated the appraising, usually disapproving, look with which he eyed them, and the soft, wet kisses that he gave, well flavored with tobacco juice. Mother found him annoying when he repeated to her gossip that he had picked up in Washington and that he vouched for as true—that President Theodore Roosevelt, for instance, was always drunk. Though his gossip produced only disapproving unbelief in Mother, he was fond of her, and this fact I account in him a virtue; it is almost the only one I was aware of. His son, George Cook Reiter, found him difficult, for Uncle George tried to run the poor fellow's life. His daughter-in-law, Helen Reiter, found him an impossible guest; he gave orders about the house as though he were still on active duty on board a battleship. She dreaded taking him on drives, for his tobacco-chewing and spitting fouled her car. Even Aunt Mamie, who loved him dearly, found his visits difficult; his smoking in her spotless house and splashing in her bathroom were almost more than she could bear. Sometime during their middle years he and Aunt Lide quarreled; though I have forgotten the cause of the quarrel, I know that he gave the provocation. His selfish disregard of other people reached its climax in his second marriage. When he was an old man and had built himself a house in California, he needed a housekeeper, and so he looked up an elderly widow whom he had known years before and married her. The marriage lasted for about a year; then he as callously left poor sentimental Aunt Theresa as he had looked her up in the first place, and resumed his bachelor life. He died in the early 1930s I think while he was paying his daughter-in-law a visit in Canton, Ohio (his son had been killed in a motor accident a few years before), and I think no one really lamented his passing.

Mammy Lettice

I cannot leave the Reiters without saying a word about Mammy Lettice, who brought Uncle George Reiter's baby son north after the mother's death. Since she was not a relative, she does not properly belong in this chapter, but she was so closely tied to the Reiters that no account of them would be complete without her.

With Lettice to help her, Aunt Lide took charge of the little George Cook Reiter. When he ceased to need her, Lettice came to the Achesons to work. Mother's tales of her behavior lead me to believe that in her youth she was something less than a treasure. Grandmother Acheson would ask Lettice to brush her hair. After a few strokes of the brush Lettice would say, "Will you excuse me for just a moment, Mrs. Acheson?" When the moment had stretched to half an hour, someone sent to fetch Lettice would find her sound asleep under a bed. Once she hid a glass goblet in Grandfather's bed just for a joke, and he was considerably startled to meet it, cold and lumpy, under the covers. She would pull out her short fuzzy hair, put powder on her very black face, and chase the Acheson children, to their great delight. Another of her tricks she used to play on the Spencer children when they were small. She would brush her hand across nose or ears and miraculously produce a shoe button from these improbable hiding places, or pluck a flower from the top of her head. We did not know her of course until she was a middle-aged woman and had left the follies of youth behind her. By that time her hair was too short to pull out (she told me once that "de Lord borned me wif bobbed hair") and she behaved more sedately, but she was always a card. This story, which belongs to the more sedate years, shows a spirit untouched by time. She was sent upstairs one evening to tell Rear Admiral Bucky Sands that dinner was ready. Very quickly she came downstairs again, her eyes rolling. Admiral Sands, she said, was saying his prayers. When asked how she knew, she answered that when she went into his room he yelled, "God damn you, close the door and get out."

After the Achesons ceased to need her, Mammy was nurse in various Pittsburgh families. Uncle Mark in her later years became her man of business. Her calls upon him always disrupted his office. She would appear in the doorway dressed in a blouse made of an old sugar sack and a woolen skirt so full itself and hung over so many petticoats that we always wondered how many inches lay between Mammy and the outside air, bob a curtsy, roll her eyes, and ask if she could see "Mr. Marcus."

When she was too old to work Uncle Mark got her into the Home for Aged and Infirm Colored Women on Lemington Avenue and looked after her interests from then until her death. At first she was not sure that she liked the home. She told me when I went to see her soon after she had taken up residence there that "Mr. Lincoln got me out of slabery, and I sold myself back in." Perhaps it was during this period that she got herself into trouble in a moment of disgruntlement by butting the matron with her woolly head. Uncle Mark had to intervene more than once at first, to placate authority when her behavior had been more than usually outrageous. In time, however, Mammy came to enjoy the home and the companionship of the other old women who shared it with her. She was perhaps helped in her adjustment by the children in the school next door. Through her window she could look into a schoolroom, and there she would stand making faces at the children until she had them in stitches. Then, feeling that she had done her boy scout good deed for the day, she would go downstairs to help in the kitchen. Food she greatly enjoyed, especially rabbit, though how without a tooth in her head she could chew, we never could understand. "I just gums it," she said, when we asked her how she managed. Mother used to buy her a rabbit occasionally, cook it at home, and take it out to her in a glass jar. Mammy's eyes rolled with joy when she saw this toothsome gift.

The bond between Mammy and the Reiters remained strong till the end. Though she could neither read nor write, she somehow managed to keep in touch. She always came to call on "Miss Lide" when Aunt Lide was in Pittsburgh, and they would sit side by side for hours talking about the past. When Betts and I heard that Aunt Lide was dying, we went to the home to pick up Mammy and take her to the cottage in Coraopolis to pay our last visit. I can still see that final scene: the pallid old woman in the bed, the little black old woman in a chair holding the white hand in her black one. And when we left, Aunt Lide, who was beyond speech, tried to wave her hand.

Mammy lived till 1932, I think. Mother was away at the time, and so when word came that Mammy was dying, Uncle Mark and I drove out to the home and were with her when she breathed her last. Mrs. Arrott and Elizabeth were there too. After it was all over, we conferred about funeral arrangements. Mrs. Arrott asked what Mammy should wear; I said I thought she should be dressed in one of her usual blouses and full skirts. "Oh no," said Elizabeth. "I promised her that she should have a white shroud." Mammy had often said that in a white dress she looked like a fly in a saucer of cream, and that's the way she looked at her funeral. It was a touching funeral, held in the parlor of the home, the mourners a handful of white friends and a roomful of old colored women who, though obviously enjoying the funeral, must have seen in it a vision of their own end. The choir boys from the Episcopal church Mammy attended were there to sing hymns to her. When it was all over we drove her to the Sewickley cemetery on the top of a high hill, and there we left her in a grave that faced the river in the valley below. She had bought and paid for her grave years before and had had a stone erected at its head marked with her name, Lettice Adams, and the date of her birth. All that had to be added was the date on which her life ended.

The Spencers

Our Spencer relatives, though less accessible than the Achesons and the Reiters, were perhaps more exciting because of their very inaccessibility. We had to travel all day or all night to reach their house in East Orange, New Jersey, and we found long journeys thrilling. Almost as exciting as going to see them was their coming to see us, for they always arrived laden with gifts. The arrival of their trunks caused an excitement impossible for the young to conceal.

Father's two sisters, Aunt Annie and Aunt Emma, we knew much better than we knew the older generation. Though Aunt Annie died while we were still children, we were old enough to remember her well. She had a flair for clothes that Mother made the most of when the aunts came to see us. She it was who helped Mother design and make for me the little red coat with shoulder capes that first I and then my younger sisters wore for years. On one visit she made a hat, for Adeline I think, which when finished she placed on a gas bracket in the spare room. When night came, some one unaware of this fact and unable to see in the dark lighted the gas, and the hat went up in smoke and flames.

Of their early visits to us I remember only a few unusual events, but our visits to them after they moved to South Orange are among the high spots of our childhood. Father, when he had to go East—I suppose on business—sometimes took one of us with him to visit his sisters. I remember with great pleasure excursions they took us on to New York—shopping expeditions in the Twenty-third Street district, visits to the Eden Musée, and demoralizingly pleasant wanderings through Schwartz's enchanting toy store.

Father's brothers and their families we seldom saw during our early years. Once when we were quite young Uncle Bob, Aunt Florence, and their two children paid us a visit. The only thing I remember about it is that Catherine and Lane called their parents Father and Mother and that after their departure we dropped Papa and Mama and followed their example.

From the very beginning of our acquaintance with her, Aunt Emma has been close to us, a fact that is indicated by the name by which she is known to all of her nephews and nieces. Aunt Emma, shortened by Uncle Wilbur's children to Tomma, has been Tomma to us all for many years. When Grandmother and Aunt Annie died within a few years of each other and Tomma was left alone, her house in South Orange became another home to her young relatives. They came to her to spend vacations from boarding school and college, to recuperate from operations, to recover after childbirth. Once I spent a whole winter with her. Whenever any of us have needed her during the years she has opened her home to us, and when we have been in trouble at home, she has come to Pittsburgh. The bond between her and us is far stronger than the usual bond between aunt and nieces and nephews; she has been to us all a dearly loved elder sister—the kind of aunt that makes us feel that we have been peculiarly blessed in our relatives.

Growing Up

Though relatives were an integral part of life during our childhood, they were not, since they were mostly grown-ups, on quite the same level of importance as the friends of our own age with whom we played every day. Amberson Avenue has always been a neighborhood of children. When we were young it supplied playmates for every one of the seven Spencers. Next door to us the Macbeths lived, so close that we could talk across the space between our side windows. Whiskery Mr. Macbeth we didn't know very well and Cousin Kate, his wife, we found alarming, but Helen was Adeline's close friend, and fat little red-haired George, Mark's contemporary, was one of the gang. Across the street lived the Reeds. Dave Reed was too old to interest us; but Jimmy, though Adeline's age, sometimes played toy soldiers with Mark, and Pussy was best friend of both Kate and Adeline. I yearned to play with these "big gales," but being three years younger than the youngest of them, I was seldom tolerated. Occasionally they let me tag along, and I still remember with keen pleasure the joy of raiding Mrs. Reed's refrigerator with them. It was there that I learned to eat olives, for the olive bottle was the chief aim of our raids—and sugar lumps, Kate says. Once when we had retreated to our own cellar with our spoils, a severe thunder storm occurred. Having heard that lightning strikes steel, I shook with terror lest divine wrath should strike me dead for the stealing in which I had just taken so enjoyable a part.

My own chief playmate was Ruth Edwards, who lived two doors above us in what later became the Lincoln house. Since she was my own age, she seemed less desirable to me than the "big gales," but we were great friends in our early years. I remember that once Mrs. Edwards sent me home because of some criminal deed Ruth and I had perpetrated. Mother found me sitting on Father's tool chest in the side hall weeping bitterly, and when she asked me the cause of my grief I told her that Mrs. Edwards had sent me home and that "she did it in her snippiest manner." We were still children when the snippy Mrs. Edwards and her family moved to Devonshire Street, and from then on Ruth and I saw less of each other, though we remained friends till the end of her life.

Closer to home, next door to us across a considerable stretch of adjoining lawn, the Snyders lived when we were very young. Billy and Mary Snyder were early playmates. Billy, I remember, had a green felt-covered board on which he kept a collection of presidential-campaign buttons that I greatly admired. Another memory of that early friendship belongs to the Snyder nursery, where Billy, demonstrating a football tackle, ran head on into my face and gave me a painfully lacerated mouth. In the nursery lived a parrot that took a fancy to my name and used to scream "Epps" as a regular accompaniment to our play. We did our first ice-skating in a flooded square at the far end of the Snyder's long back yard, but I do not remember it with pleasure since I never learned to stand up on my skates. The Snyders did not remain our neighbors for very long, and their departure ended our friendship.

When they left Amberson Avenue the McClintocks moved into the old frame house next door to us. It was a lucky day for the Spencers when in 1898 they became our neighbors. Bowdoin and Frank were too much older than the small fry to be of any use to them and too young and too socially unwilling to be of any use to our older sisters; friendship with them came later. But almost instantaneous friendship developed between the three youngest McClintocks and the Spencers. I remember tentative approaches across the honeysuckle fence that resulted at once in Mary's and Madeleine's becoming inseparable. Our twins and Rodman, whom they renamed Rob, became triplets; Kenneth, Mark, and I were still young enough to play with the younger children and, though less closely knit, were part of the gang.

From almost the day of their arrival on Amberson Avenue if the McClintocks were not at our house, we were at theirs. We crawled back and forth constantly between the wires and the honeysuckle vines that separated the two properties. Frequently one of us was invited to dine at the other's house. On such occasions the prospective guest before committing himself carefully found out the menu at each house and declined or accepted the invitation in accordance with the relative merits of the two dinners. When Rob came to our house as Betts's guest she permitted no one but herself to ask him what he wanted. Since he was always completely silent, she apparently read his thoughts, for without any exchange of words she would announce that "Rob wants some potatoes"—or steak or ice cream. Nothing enraged her more than to have anyone else ask him what he would like to eat. I remember her once being sent from the table in disgrace for storming with fury because one of us had made some polite inquiry of the silent guest.

There were so many children in the McClintock and Spencer families that other friends were hardly needed, although Father's pictures show us playing sometimes with other children. Tippy Knox, a contemporary of mine, at one time came to our house frequently. His sailor blouse, anchored firmly around his waist by an elastic, was always bulging with long sticks of black licorice. Sitting with us of an evening in the library, a string of the horrid stuff hanging from his mouth, he would quietly inhale licorice without even a pause for breath. That he came to no good end was perhaps due to his having blackened his insides too generously in his youth; Tippy and the other stray children who played with us were all right in their way, but it was our immediate neighbors who were really vital to our happiness.

Pets

Perhaps I should place among our friends the dogs that lived and played with us in our childhood and youth. The first of them I knew only as a picture in a photograph album, Gyp, Adeline's first pet. All my life I have thought that he was a pug, but Adeline assures me he was a little yellow cur. He must have gone to the happy hunting ground before I was born, for he is not even a memory to me. Nor are the kittens that Kate and Adeline spent their early childhood adopting and passionately loving, nor the chickens they tried to bring into being by sitting faithfully on a nest of eggs. I remember a canary from time to time in our nursery, but for the most part we went in for dogs rather than for heterogeneous pets.

Of all our dogs Lemmy was the most satisfactory. We came by him in this way. The summer of 1908 when we went to Bass Rocks, Massachusetts, Charles left at home in John Organ's care a cherished Irish terrier, Traddles. It was not long before the sad news came by letter that Traddles had disappeared, and Charles was heartbroken. Soon thereafter as Chick Curry was driving us through Salem we saw a man airing a mother Boston terrier and a large litter of enchanting puppies. Adeline promptly determined to have one of them for Charles, and so we either followed the man home or came back the next day to find him. I remember well the bargaining that took place: Adeline pointed out that since the puppy would have to travel all the way from Massachusetts to Western Pennsylvania, he would certainly die before he reached Pittsburgh and that it would therefore be absurd of the owner to ask very much for him. Convinced against his better judgment, he let her have the least desirable dog of the litter for five dollars. I think the puppy, although pedigreed, was the wrong color, or the wrong shape; anyway something was so wrong about him that we named him Lemon. A popular song that year ran something like this:

> Will someone kindly tell me,
> Will someone tell me why,
> To me it is a secret
> And will be till I die—
> With a million peaches round me
> Why, I should like to know,
> Did I pick a lemon in the garden of love
> Where they say only peaches grow?

While that song was popular, everybody and everything in any way undesirable was a lemon, and thus Charles's dog came by his name. Why-Why came by his because of our habit of saying, "Why, why, why, what a nice little doggie!" when the sometimes white, but more often filthy, little creature jumped up barking and screaming with joy to welcome us when we came into the house. Father used to suffer when, buying licenses for our dogs, he had to give their names as Lemon and Why-Why.

Lemmy lived to the ripe old age of fourteen. In his last years he became rheumatic and nearly blind, but when he died we all felt sad. One Sunday after a drive to Coraopolis we came home to an apparently empty house. On such occasions Lemmy usually met us at the front door with a guilty look that told us he had spent our absence on a forbidden bed or chair. We found him lying in the laundry partially paralyzed. He tried hard to wag his tail, but there was no wag left in the poor little dog. And so we summoned a vet, who quickly brought to an end a life that had meant a great deal to all of us. We took Lemmy to the country the next day and buried him beneath the cherry trees below the porch of our cottage. Mother said that she had spent a large part of her life taking care of dogs and that she wanted no more, and so Lemmy was our last canine friend.

Games

The children of our neighborhood tended to gather at 719 to play, for Mother during the day allowed us the freedom of the house, and in every other house we were confined to the nursery. Perhaps it was because we had to be repressed in the evenings when our nervous father was at home that she allowed us to tear all over the house by day. Though her patience must often have been tried, I never remember her interfering with our play. Adeline's Princess Irene game was probably the first of the many uncomfortable games with which she put up. It was inspired by George Macdonald's *The Princess and the Goblin*, which each of us in turn adored. In that book Irene's great-great-great-grandmother, who lived in the castle tower, caused an invisible thread to touch Irene's fingers and guide her to safety whenever danger threatened. Adeline as the Princess Irene would crouch behind a pile of boxes in the attic conversing with her great-great-great-grandmother; then instructed by her she would purloin spools of thread from the sewing machine and spin spiderwebs all over the house to guide her through dangers lurking in dark corners. Unwarned, a caller might easily have become entangled in this unexpected network.

More alarming would have been his sensations had he arrived on a day when we were playing spider-cow. This, the most exciting of all our indoor games, was the invention of Kate. It was hide-and-seek in reverse; instead of someone who was "it" having to find the members of the gang that had gone into hiding, the spider-cow hid and the gang ran from attic to cellar first trying to find and then trying to escape from the monster. When one least expected him to appear, he would spring from some hiding hole, flinging a wet wash cloth at his victims, and chase them all over the house. The screams and scamperings that followed his damp emergence would have shattered anyone's nerves but Mother's.

Not many of our games were as noisy as spider-cow, but some of them were even more damaging to the neatness and order. Dust-sheet houses were likely to upset a whole room for days at a time. A dust sheet was a big calico square used to cover furniture when the maid swept a room. Before the days of vacuum sweepers, straw brooms were used to clean the wall-to-wall carpets tacked down all over the house. Dampened newspapers cut in strips were thrown on the floor to catch the dust, and the vigorous sweeping with a broom that followed raised clouds of dust, against which the dust sheets protected the furniture. When not in legitimate use, they served us admirably for building purposes. We stretched them across corners and tied them to any available projections. The big bay window in the room that became Mary and Betts's, shut off from the rest of the room by a dust sheet, made the cosiest possible house for young housekeepers.

Mother must have been relieved when we played quietly in the third-floor playroom. Here the *pièce de résistance* was the miniature kitchen stove installed for Adeline and Kate when they were very young and enjoyed by each of the younger children in turn. Natural gas made it work just like the real stove in the kitchen, and in its oven and on its top we cooked many a strange mess. Cookies cut out of dough with a thimble and baked in Lilliputian pans were what I liked best to make. Pans and other pieces of kitchen equipment we kept in a long wooden box that stood against one wall. Our dishes lived in two little china closets, one of which had come from the office of our doctor great-grandfather, and both were big enough to be of real use. On their shelves sat tea sets, little plates, red glass pitchers with our names etched on them, and various other bits of glass and china dear to our hearts.

Sometimes we did our cooking in the kitchen, especially when bread was being made there. Mother would give whatever child was "helping" her a dab of dough to knead. When grimy little fingers had completed the task, a tiny gray loaf went into the oven with the big loaves, and the maker thereof smacked his lips over it at the next meal. Once Adeline made a pan of baby cinnamon rolls, which emerged from the oven sticky, sweet, and toothsome and were left on the kitchen table to cool. Presently Mollie, aware of an ominous silence, began to look about the house for trouble and found plump little Mary in the kitchen in the act of swallowing the last roll. The concoctions we cooked on the little stove in the playroom were less delicious but less of a strain on the digestion.

In earlier days the gable room was strictly a playhouse. One of its pieces of furniture was a miniature refrigerator, given to me one Christmas by Grandfather. Though a thrilling present at the moment, I found it in the end more bother than it was worth. The piece of ice carried by freezing hands from cellar to attic and bestowed in the ice compartment of the tiny icebox always melted more rapidly than I expected and overflowed the drain pan that I forgot to empty, and the milk in the food compartment turned sour before I remembered to dispose of it. We very soon ceased to use the icebox.

The other furnishings of the playhouse had more enduring value. The little painted bureau with a mirror that had belonged to Mother and that went in time to Coraopolis to hold Eleanor Nimick's doll clothes, stood against one wall. Against another wall Adeline's first playhouse stood, a heavy wooden house of a single gable made by a local carpenter, the whole front of which opened on hinges. Inside were three floors of tiny rooms, carpeted, and filled with miniature furniture. We didn't use it often, but we liked having it there. One or two small bentwood chairs and a bed or two and bureau for small dolls stood about the little room. The most interesting piece of furniture was a four-poster bed, probably of cherry wood, big enough to hold an outsize doll or a small-size baby.

This enchanting bed, although it was never regarded as mine, came into the family because of me. One day when I was a baby, Mother took her three little girls to Allegheny to call upon Aunt Isabel, the wife of her great-uncle Henry Reiter. When she arrived she discovered to her horror that she had come without any diapers. All she could do was to take the baby to the bathroom at frequent intervals and hope for the best. The baby responded superbly to this treatment and returned home a dry girl. Aunt Isabel was so impressed by the infant's super intelligence that she gave to the three children the doll bed that her own children had played with. It is a solidly built bed with a piece of rope woven across for springs—so solid and so capacious that it can hold a real baby. My two big sisters liked to put me on it, Mother said, and, given many years later to Eleanor Nimick, it has held baby Nimicks too. Now Marnie Nimick goes to sleep across it, half in and half out, sharing its comfort with her teddy bears.

In our day we tucked dolls, not bears, under its covers. We all had dolls, which we played with more or less. I remember buying dolls with great pleasure at Lauer's toy store with money hoarded for the purpose, and delighting in their flaxen curls and eyes that opened and closed. After our twins were born we went in for twin dolls, and the playhouse positively swarmed with twins in long dresses. I have vivid memories of harrowing games with Mary Gordon during which our children became desperately ill and died in spite of their young mothers' devoted ministrations. Mary Spencer was given to very dramatic doll-playing, but in the main I satisfied my maternal instinct by making my children clothes.

We all of us loved to paint. Perhaps Adeline was our inspiration, for she, with some real talent and a little training at the School of Design, painted and drew pictures that we regarded as masterpieces of beauty. Every child had his own paint box in which he could mess about to his heart's content. Mary, more enterprising than the rest of us, in her extreme youth once purloined from Adeline's room a cherished white plaster Venus and painted it gold. Though this use of paint was not encouraged, our paint boxes were a never failing source of pleasure to us.

Another favorite form of entertainment was dressing up, sometimes in each other's clothes, but more often in the discarded finery of our elders. I think that Grandmother Spencer and the aunts sent clothes they had finished with to Mother to be cut over into dresses for us and that those unsuitable for this purpose were given to us to play with. I remember with particular affection a gray tea gown that must have been already ancient when it came to us, for its soft silk was slitting. As I remember it, its tightly fitted and heavily boned bodice had a pale blue shirred front and its skirt had a trailing train that we liked to swish about behind us. Though few of our costumes were as elegant as this, we had a large assortment of ancient relics to choose from when we wanted to dress up.

Whom we became in these glamorous clothes depended upon whose was the master mind directing the game. Kate as a plump little girl liked to be transformed into Queen Victoria; Mary and Elizabeth, less royal in their ambitions, often turned themselves into boys. We all enjoyed on occasions becoming someone quite different from ourselves in plays composed sometimes by as distinguished an author as Shakespeare and sometimes improvised by the actors themselves on the stage. Kate and Adeline in the days before I can remember did a scene from *Romeo and Juliet*. Adeline as Romeo wooed a Juliet (Kate) clad in a flowing white nightgown, her brown curls bobbing as she leaned over her balcony (the dining room table) to ask soulfully, "Romeo, Romeo, wherefore art thou Romeo?" Kate also frequently gave a solo performance in which standing on the taboret that customarily held a jardiniere containing a withering palm she asked the audience, "What is so good as a hearty good laugh?" and then illustrated her text so fervently that she nearly fell off the taboret.

The only playwright among us was Mark, who at one point in

his early career was a diligent dramatist. The most famous of his plays, *The Dear Little Witch of a Dorothy,* not even the author can now remember very much about. I have a faint recollection of the dear little witch emerging unexpectedly from the middle cupboard of the massive dining room sideboard, and Charles remembers that during a duel scene in which one of the characters was killed the problem of how to dispose of the body was solved by throwing it into the garbage can. Perhaps it was in this play that Kenneth McClintock, costumed in the gray silk tea gown, proved more memorable than the part he played. The swishing train, the stiffly boned bodice, the blue shirred front topped by a masculine face and closely clipped curls no one could easily forget.

Our audiences were made up of relatives and neighbors—of anyone, in fact, whom we could persuade to come and who was willing to pay the entrance fee of a pin. To our immense disgust we were not allowed to charge real money for our shows. On one occasion I think we were permitted to levy tribute on the audience for the Childrens Hospital, but never, alas, for ourselves.

Not all our playing took place indoors. Out-of-doors it was divided into what might be called casual play and formal games. There was, for instance, the pursuit of the ice wagon, which occurred whenever the ice wagon hove in sight. All the children would gather about the ice man as he broke an enormous cake of ice with his pick into pieces of a size to fit into refrigerators. We watched with admiration his feats of strength as he lifted up huge chunks with his tongs and carried them into the house. The minute his back was turned we began to scrabble about with the chips of ice at the open end of the wagon, trying to find pieces the right size for our mouths. When the ice man returned and drove away, there was always a fringe of children hanging to the back of the wagon.

Returning from ice-wagon excursions, we might occupy ourselves by sliding down the cellar door or climbing trees. Adeline and Helen Macbeth played house in our apple trees, and I remember with pleasure pulling myself to great heights in them and feeling the pride of conquest. The apple trees must have died early, for they soon disappeared. The two sour-cherry trees that remained were perfect for small children, but baby stuff for ambitious climbers. Even Lemmy, our dog, could climb the one cherry tree that survived into our maturity. More challenging were the tall sweet-cherry trees that flanked Grandfather's house. We swarmed over them in cherry season, baskets slung over our arms. None of us can ever forget the heavenly joy of eating the first cherries of the season or the horrid check to joy when we met the first worm. We would come down from the trees with black faces well smeared with cherry juice and baskets full of big black cherries, the best, I am sure, that ever grew.

Another of our outdoor activities was gardening, though it is not one at which we were very successful. I remember planting seeds again and again that never produced a single green shoot, probably because the zealous gardener planted them practically in China. We were more successful with the pansies Mother brought home from the market in the spring. These plants, already well developed, were able to survive our loving care for some time, and they gave us enormous pleasure.

Our digging was not always the constructive digging of the gardener. All of us, I think, except perhaps Kate and Adeline who had outgrown their digging days before I knew them, liked to dig in the hole between the cellar door and the Macbeth house. It was a lovely hole, capable of becoming anything that the imagination desired—a tunnel, a cave, a lake, a house, a zoo. . . . It also furnished ammunition for mud throwers. I cannot remember whether mud throwing was ever one of my own sins, but Charles, Betts, and Rob McClintock enjoyed firing mud balls at the Macbeths' kitchen windows.

In summer one of our favorite diversions was playing with water. Clad in our bathing suits we took turns sitting on the sprinkler and squirting each other with the hose. This was a delightful game; it kept us amiable and pleasantly damp through days of unbearable heat. In such weather our costume during dry hours was scantier than it was when we were clad in heavy all-enveloping woollen bathing suits. Indoors and even in the privacy of the back yard we scampered about clad only in our underwear—"panty body waists" to which our muslin drawers were neatly buttoned. Father's pictures include some ravishing ones of his children in hot-weather costumes.

The boys of the neighborhood often played hockey in the street. I never liked this game because I always got banged by their hockey sticks, but Betts took to it like a duck to water and played with tomboy enthusiasm. All of us loved to dash about on roller skates. With the first spring day out came the skates and the air was filled with the music of wheels clicking over cracks in flagstone sidewalks. Up the street to the church, along the broad path that led to the church steps, around the church porch to Westminster Place, along Westminster to Amberson, and then a glorious coast down the street to our house—the memory of roller-skating in spring still stirs me. I quite fancied myself as a skater and remember distinctly enjoying my own grace as I clattered down the Amberson Avenue pavement. Jumping rope was fun too, but it did not give one quite such an opportunity for self-admiration.

Very often when we were out-of-doors we played conventional games. Ten Steps was always both a favorite game and the cause of tears and conflict. Someone who was "it" sat on the McClintocks' front steps with his eyes closed; the rest of us stood with one foot touching the bottom step and the other ready for flight the minute "it" began to count. He counted up to ten as fast or as slowly as he pleased while the rest of us ran up the broad brick walk as far as we could before he finished counting. When he said "Ten," we had to be motionless; if he saw anyone moving he called the poor wretch back to begin again. It was at this point that the tears began to flow; the offender denied having moved; "it" insisted he had seen motion. I don't know why we liked this game, for it always ended in a fight.

The game I remember with greatest joy is Prisoners' Base. I think it may have been the first game I was ever allowed to play with "the big gales," and so to this day it is touched for me with romance. Two captains chose "sides," and the two groups then took their stands on opposite sides of the street. Then the members of each group would prance out from base trying to tempt their enemies to come out and be caught. When after much dodging a member of one team succeeded in catching a member of the other team, he brought his prisoner to home base. The prisoner with one foot on the enemy curb and his hand outstretched, waited until a member of his own team slipped through defenses and freed him by touching his outstretched hand.

The only game that ever gave me more joy than Prisoners' Base was a farming game I played just once with Kate and the twins—Kate's last day of childish play, Mother said. It began with grass cutting. Kate pushed the lawn mower, and the twins and I raked the fallen grass into piles. While it was drying, we built a hay loft in a triangular corner between the bicycle shed and the wall of the house. At that point the twins were transformed into ponies and hitched to Mark's red express wagon, which on the instant became a hay wagon into which Kate and I loaded the hay. The ponies pulled it to the barn, and the farmers pitched it into the loft. If this game marked the end of Kate's childhood, it marked the high point of mine.

Illness

Sometimes the orderly routine of our days was interrupted by illness. Except for Mark, who was far from robust, we were all reasonably healthy children, but in the days when there were no preventive serums we had all the normal diseases of childhood. And because there were seven of us, a disease, once started, often swept through the family knocking us down like ten pins one after another. Usually by some perversity of fate only three or four would succumb at one time, leaving the rest to be smitten inconveniently some years later. I remember once that Mary, determined to catch whatever the disease was, ate from the same spoon as Mark, who had already broken out in spots, but remained healthy in spite of these heroic measures. But ultimately, whether together or singly, we suffered through whooping cough, chicken pox, mumps, and measles. We had every known kind of measles—the real thing, German, three day. Someone was always developing a rash and having to go into retirement.

Cousin John Wishart (a cousin of Grandfather Acheson's) remained our doctor until the only really serious illness any of us ever had in childhood nearly brought Mary's life to an end when

The seven Spencer children with Mother and Father, September 1900.

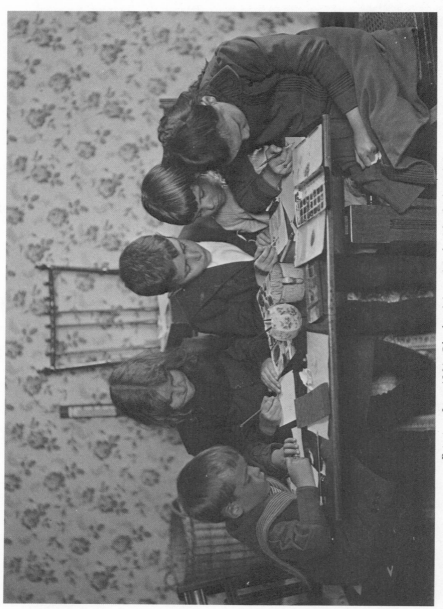

Painting, June 1901: Charles, Mary, Mark, Elizabeth, Ethel.

Happy play scene in Mary and Elizabeth's room, October 1903.

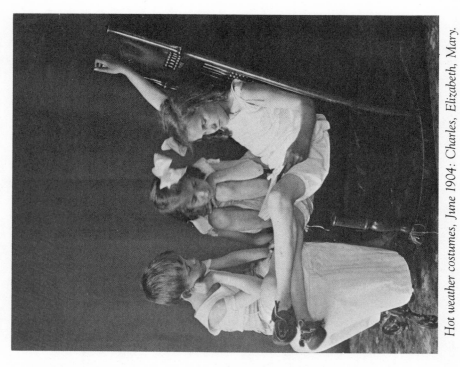

Hot weather costumes, June 1904: Charles, Elizabeth, Mary.

Kate and Fluffy, November 1899.

Hot weather costumes, June 1898: Elizabeth, Ethel, Charles, Mary, Kate, Mark. Mark, the delicate one, was not allowed to shed his clothes.

Sliding down the cellar door, July 1901: Elizabeth, Mary, Charles.

The digging hole, November 1901: Charles, Mary, Rodman McClintock,
Elizabeth Totten, Elizabeth.

Playing in the backyard, July 1900: Mary, Kenneth McClintock, Mark, Madeleine
McClintock, Tippy Knox, Charles, Elizabeth, George Macbeth.

Mary and Elizabeth in the sick chair, May 1906.

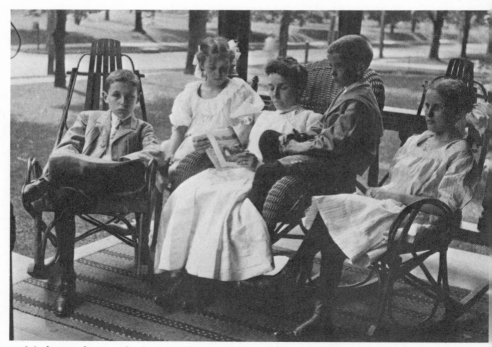

Mother reading on the front porch, July 1905: Mark, Elizabeth, Mother, Charles, Mary.

she was seven years old. She came down with diphtheria shortly before Christmas. I think it was not so diagnosed at first, for on Saturday night Kate and I went to dancing school as usual. But when Molly came for us, to our great surprise she took us to Grandfather's house instead of to our own. There we found Adeline already established, and there we three stayed for weeks while the rest of the family, Father excepted, remained in quarantine. How he came to be allowed to go to work from a quarantined house I do not know.

The doctor came to Grandfather's house and gave the three Spencer girls each a shot of antitoxin, which I think was new at that time. It made us so stiff that we could hardly get up the next morning, but our brief misery was as nothing to the misery the family was enduring at home. The twins developed chicken pox and were put to bed and cared for by Mollie. The trained nurse brought in to take care of Mary promptly came down with diphtheria herself and departed, and Mother, shut away from the rest of the family in Mary's room, had to nurse a child who became sicker and sicker. Cousin John, I think, finally suggested that a younger man be called in consultation, and Ogden Edwards, then a promising young doctor at the beginning of his career, took over. Diphtheria was the prime killer of children in those days, and poor little Mary had almost reached her end. Her fingers were cold and bloodless, her lips were blue, her nose was pinched, and she was gasping for breath when Dr. Edwards after several futile attempts finally succeeded in dropping a tube down her throat and getting air into her lungs.

I remember vividly that night when death seemed about to strike our family for the first time. Though no one had told me how serious Mary's condition was, I must have felt the tension in the air, for when we three girls, all together in the guest room, went to bed, I began to cry, and soon Adeline and Kate raised their voices too in lamentation. It was the first time sorrow had touched us. When morning came and with it the news that Mary was better, even the little ten year old who had started the concerted weeping felt the relief of her elders.

The convalescence was long and slow. From it Mary emerged

shot full of hypodermic punctures, her voice curiously husky, but with appetite and energy unimpaired. What with belated Christmas presents and the gifts that had been showered upon her during convalescence, the small invalid thoroughly enjoyed herself.

We were lucky enough to get through childhood without any operations, and Mark was the only one of us to have an accident more serious than the bumps, bruises, and cuts that every child experiences. During a game at school one of the players tackled him so hard that he fell with a thump that broke his right arm. "When I picked myself up," he says, "my arm hurt like Hades, so I just dropped out of the game quietly and went indoors meaning to go to my desk in the study hall. However, I got no further than my locker, where the pain was unabated. . . . I put on my coat and went home, where fortunately Mother was. . . . Dr. Litchfield was sent for as soon as Mother had helped me off with my jacket. I could see the poor twisted arm with the ulna shaped like a bow instead of being straight—which comforted me that something was really the matter. I had felt a coward running away from school, and had been ashamed that I had almost cried in front of my schoolmates."

A painful setting and bandaging of the arm followed and six weeks of splints and sling. On the day the splints were removed during a game of tag at home with Mary and the twins Mark fell and broke the arm a second time. Since the first setting had not restored the bone to completed straightness, this catastrophe was perhaps a well-disguised blessing. The second setting was entirely successful and in six more weeks the arm emerged as good as new.

Diphtheria and broken bones were too serious to have left happy memories, but when our upsets were milder the period of recuperation at least was always rather pleasant. First came the returning joy of eating. I loved the salty, meaty taste of the beef broth that Mother made for the invalid. Mark, I remember, always wanted an egg first of all. From the market Mother brought tender little squabs to tempt the appetite of the patient and make him feel important. Meals were served on the "sick table," a table designed to open up across a bed. We used it not only for meals but for play when we were sufficiently recovered to sit up. From the bed we graduated to the "sick chair," lowered for semireclining, with footrest out for invalid feet. When we were able to walk about a bit, we regained strength pumping and playing the organ, which lived in Mary and Elizabeth's room.

Best of all the joys of convalescence was being read aloud to. Natural talent and long years of practice had made Mother a champion reader. She read innumerable books to us from the time we were old enough to listen until the end of her life, but the novels of Dickens were what she loved best to read aloud. When she was a little girl her parents gave her a full set of Dickens with Cruikshank illustrations. She read the novels first to her little brothers and sisters and then in relays to her own children—to Adeline and Kate, to Ethel and Mark, to Mary and the twins. By the time the youngest Spencers had been initiated the older ones knew Dickens almost by heart and Mother herself was letter perfect. She read with enormous relish and with great dramatic skill. She would not have made a good actress; the theatre, unless the play were by Shakespeare, bored her, and acting was alien to her practical, rather literal nature. Yet nothing could have been more dramatic than her reading: her voice recorded every shade of feeling; every character spoke with his own intonations. No wonder that Dickens's novels came alive for us or that reading became our favorite pastime.

Every evening when there was no homework to be done we gathered round her in the library while she read aloud and we sewed or knitted. Often while she was thus engaged we made Christmas presents for her. Admonishing her not to look, we turned the backs of our chairs toward her and stitched away diligently while she read to the backs of our heads. In time the sound of her own voice induced sleepiness, and in that half comatose state no teetotaling lady ever sounded more drunken. But these lapses were brief, for we harried her out of them. One of the reasons we found Sundays so trying was that churchly activities cheated us out of a full quota of reading. Of all the memories of our happy relationship with our mother, her reading aloud to us, whether we were well or ill, is probably for all of us the most blessed.

Education and Religion

Education

Play, unfortunately we thought, was too often interrupted by far less important activities. Of these school, of course, was the most time-consuming. The education of their seven children posed a problem for our parents, but unaware of the speed with which their family would grow, they started off their two eldest in aristocratic fashion. Adeline and Kate began their schooling with a German governess named Fräulein Turk, who conducted a private class, sometimes in the home of Dr. Holland, sometimes at the Reed's across the street from us, and sometimes at our house. Kate remembered sitting in our dining room under the clock while Fräulein Turk introduced her to the German language. The pupils were Raymond and Moorhead Holland, Pussy and Jimmy Reed, Adeline Spencer, and, for part of one year at least, Kate Spencer. Adeline must have been very young and Kate little more than an infant, but whatever Kate may or may not have accomplished, Adeline learned to read and write German script. The chief thing she remembers of this first educational experience is that Mrs. Holland promised a bird to the pupil who received the best marks. Ambitious little Adeline strained to excel and ended at the head of the class, but the bird never materialized and her disappointment has survived the years. Another trying memory is of Horace Moorhead, uncle of the Holland boys. He was what was known in our youth as "deaf and dumb," though dumbness with him had been replaced by a strange kind of inhuman speech.

When he appeared in the classroom, took Adeline on his knee, and talked to her in his sepulchral voice, she nearly died of fright.

After probably two years of this exclusive education, the two little Spencer girls entered the Alinda School on the corner of Fifth Avenue and Craig Street, where the University Square apartments now stand, a private school that enjoyed considerable prestige in its day. Adeline, who knew how to read and write English as well as German, went straight into the school proper, but Kate began operations in the kindergarten, where her popularity was so great that the little boys in her class fought each morning for the privilege of standing beside her. One boy would pound the hand of a rival who had already clasped her hand in the circle of children and by violence win the desired place by her side.

The rest of us in turn followed her to kindergarten with very real enjoyment. Since we all liked to do things with our hands, the activities were much to our taste. I myself loved all the hand work: to fold papers of enchanting colors into interesting shapes, to weave mats of incredible beauty, to make strange animals out of slimy gray clay, to build cities in the sand box. Another vivid memory has to do with being taken to kindergarten by Mollie. It must have been in her early days with us when I was experimenting to see how far I could safely go with her. I remember flinging myself down on the sidewalk of Fifth Avenue and kicking and screaming furiously and Mollie putting me on my feet again and making me understand that no such nonsense would be tolerated. It was kindergarten too that caused me to contribute my share of tears one famous morning when all seven Spencer children cried before breakfast. Adeline cried because Kate was so slow she was going to make them late to school; Kate cried because Adeline was heckling her; Mark cried because he was half sick; Mary who was not yet two, and the twins, who were babies, cried because they did not know any better; and I cried because our pictures were to be taken that day at kindergarten and I did not want to have any part in the ordeal. As a rule, however, kindergarten gave us all joy, not grief.

All of us but Adeline went to the Alinda to kindergarten, but only Adeline was a pupil in the school proper. Miss Stewart, the principal, believed in the rule of love and paid no heed to other kinds of discipline. When Adeline came home one day and reported that the rule of love had resulted in the more enterprising pupils locking Miss Stewart in her office, from which she had had to escape by climbing out of a window, Father and Mother decided to look for a school with a less loving headmistress. Hearing that Miss Elizabeth Fundenberg was the best elementary teacher in Pittsburgh, they switched Adeline and Kate to the Osceola School when Kate was ready for the first grade (she was almost immediately promoted to the second), and there in due course the rest of us followed our big sisters.

It was a public school, but small and in a sufficiently residential section of the city to supply us with suitable companions. By the time the Spencers got there Miss Fundenberg had been made principal, and so none of us enjoyed the benefit of her teaching. She seemed to us a stern, unapproachable woman, but I think she must have been a good administrator. Her second in command in my day was Miss Ruswenkel—Miss Rustyfinger we called her—about whom I remember only that she had shoe-button black eyes and glossy black hair and that she was tall, massive, and terrifying.

On the whole it was a good school. There were some poor teachers, to be sure. Miss Dickson who presided over Room 10, which she called Osceola College, murdered the King's English, though I think she knew how to teach arithmetic. Miss Skelly, the second-grade teacher, had bright red hair and a flaming temper. I remember nothing of what she taught us, but she put the fear of the Lord into her small charges. I always shook in my boots when she dragged a misbehaving little boy into the cloak room and whacked him with a ruler. Most of our teachers did their jobs well, and some of them won both our respect and our devotion. I remember Miss Reese of Room 1 as the person who taught me most of what I know about phonetics. Miss Petty, in Room 6, taught me how to spell and pronounce the queer combination of letters that make the word *weigh*. Someone in those early grades taught me to tell the difference between left and right; left was the side next the blackboard when we were lined up ready to march out of the room at the end of the day. I still tend to think myself back to that blackboard when I have to distinguish between left and right. In the upper grades, Miss Macmillan and Miss McComb stand out as exceptionally good teachers. At the Osceola School we were well drilled in the fundamentals, and our ambition was stirred.

We never received rewards, however, for doing well in school; no bright silver dollars came to us for good reports, as they came to some of our friends. Our parents expected us to reach the top of our classes, and sometimes we did. Kate, I think, always did; her quick mind solved problems so swiftly that she did them on her slate, rubbed them out, and did them over again two or three times before the other children had finished doing them once. The rest of us achieved the degree of distinction that our abilities and application entitled us to.

My personal initiation to school was disillusioning. Always in my very early days I yearned to be like the "big gales" and to do everything they did, and because they went to school I burned with envious desire to do likewise. When I was six and entitled to enter the public school system Mother would have kept me out another year, feeling that I was still too little a girl to be put into captivity. Since she herself had not started to school till she was ten, she thought there was no good reason for children beginning so young. But when I begged and pleaded to be allowed to go she finally relented, warning me however that if once I started, on I should have to go, that having put my hand to the plough I should not be permitted to turn back. It took only a day of captivity to disillusion me, but since Mother was a woman of her word, it was useless to argue with her, and I had to resign myself to being educated. My unhappiness was rendered greater by my big sisters during those early days of schooling. Since I was only six, it was their duty as experienced travelers to escort me to school and bring me home again. Every once in so often they forgot this unwelcome responsibility, and when they got home, Mother sent them back to fetch me. Down Amberson Avenue, up the McKay hill, across Center Avenue to Cypress Street, up Cypress Street to the school they stamped in a fury to collect an equally infuriated little sister, and together the three stamped home shooting off sparks of fire as they went.

Year by year the army of Spencers tramping that journey to school grew. Adeline and Kate had finished at the Osceola before the twins were old enough to start, but for a year at least five of us made the daily journey together either on foot or on our bicycles. When we rode, we were under orders to get off our bikes at every streetcar crossing, carefully scan the street for approaching danger, and when all was safe scurry across on foot. Mark used to annoy us by his excess of caution. Seeing a streetcar two good blocks away, he would wait until it had passed, by which time something else would be coming in the other direction to delay us further. There was never any danger of anyone's being run over while Mark was with us.

When the weather was very bad Grandfather sent the carriage to take us to school. We prayed for rain so that John Organ would come for us. On one such morning he had exciting news to report: a little baby had been born at his house the night before and he was thinking of naming her Ethel. As I was preening myself at the thought of having a namesake, Adeline dashed my hopes. "Oh, John," she said, "please name her for me!" Nothing if not obliging, John instantly complied, and the little black namesake became Adeline's, not mine. Thereafter John always referred to his daughter as Miss Adeline and to our sister as Adeline, a reversal of titles that at the time did not seem strange.

I do not remember our early school days very vividly; only an occasional scene stands out. The pencil sharpener on the landing of the stairs is unforgettable, probably because I had never seen anything like it before and greatly admired the pencil points it produced. It must have been a very extravagant sharpener, for it took off enormous quantities of wood and left the pencil with a long, elegantly sloping point. It gave me infinite pleasure to fix my pencil in the holder and move it gently back and forth till the point was sharp as a dagger. Once as I was waiting my turn, a big girl said, "Oh, the dickens," when her point broke. I was filled with admiration and yearned to imitate her, but since even the mildest oaths were discouraged at home, I never dared to use such vigorous expletives.

The speaker of these inspiring words was actually breaking a rule in opening her mouth at all. We were allowed to use the pencil sharpener between classes only on the understanding that we would sharpen our pencils in perfect silence. One day as Mark was waiting his turn at the sharpener with a group of chattering children, Miss Macmillan passed by and sent them to the office to be reprimanded by Miss Fundenberg. Mark she excused with these unwise words: "You can go back to your room, Mark. I know *you* were not talking." Mark, who had been chattering with the best of them, departed with hanging head. For days his conscience gnawed so painfully that he finally confessed his sin and was absolved.

There were sixteen rooms in the Osceola School, but since there are only eight grades in the elementary school system, I think that each room must originally have been intended for half a grade. In our day only ten rooms were in use, but even so we were sometimes promoted at the end of the first term and sometimes we even skipped a room. In due course each little Spencer finally reached Room 16 and left the school for other fields of learning. At this point our parents shifted each child in turn to a private school; none of us went to a public high school except Mary, who for one term attended what was called "the high-school class" at the Sterrett School, and for the second term transferred to Peabody High School because her teacher at Sterrett had "insulted" her. Why she alone of the seven was sent to high school even briefly she does not know, but I suppose the family fortunes must have been at low ebb that year.

We lived in a neighborhood where children went to private, not public, schools. Our parents, I think, felt that free education for seven children was worth a little social sacrifice and that it would not hurt us to be separated from our friends during the early years. When we reached adolescence and social life was beginning, more snobbish motives prevailed and our public schooling came to an end. When Adeline finished at the Osceola she was sent to Miss Thurston's School, which I think our parents hoped was founded on a sterner discipline than Miss Stewart's Alinda. There she and Annabel Baggley became bosom friends. When our sister was at home she spent most of her time at the telephone talking to "Belle dear." Perhaps it was these long-drawn-out conversations about boys and the general demoralization that followed transfer from the strictness of the public school to the slackness of the private that made Father and Mother think they had made a mistake; at any rate after a year they shifted Adeline from Miss Thurston's to the preparatory department of the Pennsylvania College for Women, commonly known as P.C.W. If they had hoped to get her away from Annabel they were disappointed, for Annabel went with her to P.C.W.; and if they had hoped to fill a fun-loving, popular adolescent with a passion for learning their hope was again defeated. I think that they sent her to boarding school in 1901—to the Baldwin School in Bryn Mawr—because they did not know how to cope with her at home.

None of her sisters and brothers will ever forget the joy of her return for vacations from boarding school and college. On the morning of her arrival, when enough time had elapsed for Father to have gone to the East Liberty station by streetcar and brought her and her suitcase home, the little brothers and sisters would dash up the street to Fifth Avenue to swarm about her when she stepped off the trolley, ready to laugh at her every word. When we gathered about the breakfast table after we reached home she would turn her fingers into animals that galloped entrancingly over the table, accompanying these gyrations with jokes and tales of boarding-school life that doubled us up with laughter. I think that by that time the twins had outgrown the perennial joke she played on them during their earlier years. When they, after a time-worn custom of the Spencer family, had removed the strips of icing from between the layers of their cake, meaning to eat them later as the gustatory climax of their dinner, she would cry in a tone of great excitement, "Oh, look—there's a monkey on the porch (or an elephant in the street)!" And the poor little innocents, deceived every time by the false excitement in her voice, would look. While they looked, a swift hand would make the cherished strips of icing disappear. Though they had learned by the time Adeline went to boarding school not to be deceived by such obvious bait, they still found her a miraculous and infinitely entertaining creature from another world. So did the rest of us. No big sister, I am sure, ever had a more appreciative audience.

Often when she came home for vacations she brought friends with her. These young lady guests we looked upon with admiration. In the formal age in which we grew up we had to treat them with great respect. Though they were not actually many years older than we were, Mother insisted that we address them as Miss West, Miss Swindell, Miss Tillotson. I don't think we ever questioned the propriety of this convention, but looked back upon from the mid-twentieth century when childen often call even their parents by their first names, the formality of our childhood seems ludicrous.

Whether there were guests in the house or not, there were always parties and party clothes when Adeline came home from school—and beaux too. The younger children hid behind the window curtains, giggling with excitement, to watch the comings and goings of all these fabulous creatures, their eyes round with admiration for "college men," pretty girls, pretty clothes, and black velvet boots protecting dancing slippers.

After a year at boarding school Adeline decided—or perhaps Mother and Father decided for her—to go to Bryn Mawr College, less, I think, because she wanted more education than because she liked freedom from parental supervision. A summer of tutoring with Miss Wright, who was just starting her school in Bryn Mawr, enabled Adeline to pass off an entrance condition in Roman history, but not, alas, in punctuation. She flunked the punctuation examination and left college two years later still sublimely indifferent to the functions of commas, semicolons, and periods. She entered Bryn Mawr College in September 1902. I do not think she was a very diligent student, but unquestionably she enjoyed life. In those benighted days it was not socially the thing for a girl to go to college, and to go to Bryn Mawr College, which was regarded as extremely highbrow, was to damn oneself in the eyes of all right-thinking young males. So for the two years Adeline spent in Bryn Mawr College she never once confessed her shame to any man; when asked, she always said she was a Baldwin girl. In 1904, when she and Chick Curry had persuaded Father and Mother to let them get married in June of 1905, she came home to prepare for matrimony, and so her education ended two years short of an A.B. degree. Happily married, the mother of eight children and the grandmother of eighteen, she told me once that she never for one split second regretted her abandonment of college.

When Kate left the Osceola School she joined Adeline at P.C.W., and there she stayed until the autumn of 1903. Then I, who had just finished at the Osceola, went with her to Miss Gleim's, a new school that had recently opened in two old double houses on the corner of Negley Avenue and Howe Street.

I do not know why Kate was sent to Miss Gleim's. It was chosen for me, I am sure, largely for convenience. Miss Mitchell's School on Braddock Avenue, though known to be good, was far away and involved the expense of carfare. Miss Gleim was a college woman, her school though new was doing well, and it was within easy walking distance of home. Kate stayed there for one year and then went for one more year to boarding school—to Miss Wright's School in Bryn Mawr, where Adeline had tutored before entering college.

Whether I learned anything at Miss Gleim's School I do not remember, but I stayed there for three years. In 1906 I followed Kate to Miss Wright's School in Bryn Mawr, and there in June, 1908, my education presumably ended; as Kate's had ended three years earlier.

Why it never occurred to anyone to send Kate to college is a mystery; she had by far the best mind in the family and was the most worth educating. Probably the basic reason for letting her stop school at eighteen was that there was no money to send her to college. By 1905 when she would have been ready to enter, Father had retired and the financial situation at home was strained. Moreover, her health was none too good; arthritis was beginning, and Mother was too intent on trying to cure her child to give much thought to her further education. Actually, college might have cured Kate by giving her the absorbing interest she needed to pull her out of her slough of despond.

Father's attitude toward college certainly had a good deal to do with the matter too. Having seen his Grandmother Jones, early widowed and left penniless, struggling to make a living by keeping a boardinghouse, and his Aunt Emma Fry in her turn forced to turn boardinghouse keeper for the same reason, Father was determined that his five little daughters should be spared this hard fate. Fortunately he married a very thrifty woman who helped him to save every possible penny and also I think to curb his own naturally extravagant tastes. It never occurred to him that it would have been better to educate his daughters so that they could make a living for themselves. Actually in the world he knew there was nothing women could do but take in boarders or teach, and so his theory of saving and investing in order that his daughters might have an income to live on in idleness made sense from his point of view.

For daughters growing up in the twentieth century, however, it was not a wise point of view, though at the age of eighteen neither Kate nor I realized that fact. I do not think that Kate wanted to go to college, and I know that I rebelled at the mere thought of it. Mother wanted me to go, insisted on my taking the college preparatory course at school, and hoped against hope that when the time came money could be found to send me. I fought furiously against her plan, for none of my friends were going to college and I wanted to be just like everybody else. In the end I won, whether because Mother felt that in that mood I would get no benefit from college or whether because the financial situation made her plan impractical I do not know. Unquestionably Kate and I would both have been better off if we had gone to college.

Mother's attitude toward higher education for women was totally different from Father's; she believed wholeheartedly in college education for girls. Kate was the only one of us for whom unaccountably she had no such ambition. She herself had gone to college and loved it, and she wanted the experience for her daughters. It is interesting to note that after Father's death she achieved her ambition. Looking back on those years I do not see how she did it. For one year Mary, Elizabeth, Charles, and I were all in college at the same time, and Mark was in Union Theological Seminary. After Mary finished, there were still four of us draining the family resources at Smith, Cornell, Radcliffe, and Union respectively. Though college did not cost as much in 1915 as it does now, money was not plentiful at home. Mother lived very frugally and borrowed from the bank when she could not make her income stretch sufficiently to cover the cost of education. It makes me blush for shame to think how we took her skimping and saving for granted. We sent our laundry home, where she, poor dear, uncomplainingly week after week unpacked it for Minnie to wash, packed it again, and carried the boxes to the post office in East Liberty for mailing. I dare say this procedure saved money, but it was not calculated to conserve strength. And each of us, intent on his or her personal affairs, would write home asking for money. Mother never complained, cheerfully complied with our requests, and somehow managed to pay all the bills. To her no sacrifice was too great if it won for her children the education she was convinced they needed to cope with life in the twentieth century.

In this matter, as in many others, she was far ahead of her own generation. The accepted pattern for girls in our youth was to finish school, "come out," get married, and live happily ever after. For a girl who was not a social success and did not get married, who had neither society, a husband, house, nor children to occupy her, life was dull and meaningless. It took the first World War to jostle Kate out of her rut. It sent her to Carnegie Tech to take a hurry-up secretarial course and from there to Washington, D.C., to a job in the Coal Administration. After that her own intelligence carried her to increasingly interesting work with doctors—first in Washington, then in Providence, and finally in Boston, with a brief interlude spent in running a bookshop in Pittsburgh. She acquired in the course of the years the self-education that in the end is perhaps more valuable than anything college can give.

It took seven unhappy years of doing nothing more interesting than making clothes and teaching a Sunday School class to make me realize that I wanted a college education after all. The Sunday School class was particularly galling, for having decided at the age of sixteen that I was an atheist, I could not teach with any conviction. But it was expected that from my own profound ignorance I should enlighten a class of little girls, and I lacked the courage to rebel. My escape from futility came by the purest chance. One day a second cousin named Fanny Lyon, seeing me on the front porch of 719, dropped in for a moment. She had wanted very much to go to college, but her snobbish family would not hear of her doing anything so unconventional. However, they were willing to let her go to Margaret Morrison Carnegie College at Carnegie Tech to learn the household arts, and so she was devoting that year to studies for which she had not the slightest aptitude. She urged me to join her there, and Mother joined in the urging. Thus prodded, I enrolled the next day in the secretarial course, for which my aptitude was also nil. However, the English courses I took on the side showed me where my talents lay, and at the end of the year I decided to go to a liberal arts college and prepare myself for teaching. The autumn of 1915 I entered P.C.W. as a freshman, carried the full freshman load and worked off three or four entrance conditions at the same time, and at the end of the year transferred to Radcliffe College, from which I was graduated in 1919.

Mary, when she finished at the Osceola, after one year in the public high school went to Miss Mitchell's, by this time renamed the Winchester School, which had moved to Fifth Avenue and Clyde Street within easy reach of home. Elizabeth a little later followed her there. By Mary's time, though more girls were going to college than had gone in my day, the old pattern still held pretty firmly. She was expecting to come out with her friends the autumn of 1912, but when she finished school at eighteen Mother persuaded her to fill in the year that lay between her and her debut by entering P.C.W. as a freshman. When Father's death in August of 1912 put an end to the plan for coming out, Mother again persuaded her to continue her education. Feeling that it would be easier for her child to be far away while her friends were enjoying a debutante life that mourning prevented her from having, she sent Mary to Smith College. Though Mary departed reluctantly, drenched in tears, she loved college. After her graduation in 1915 she taught physics for a year at Miss Mitchell's School, followed that experience by a year as technician in the Department of

Pathology at the University of Pittsburgh School of Medicine, and then gave up her career in 1917 to marry Francis Nimick and to devote the future to husband, children, grandchildren, social activities, and gardening.

By the time Elizabeth finished school, college was a much more usual next step than it had been for her older sisters. She went to Smith without one rebellious murmur, though not, I think, with much scholarly enthusiasm. Since the first World War was going on when she emerged from college, she followed Kate's example and took the hurry-up secretarial course at Carnegie Tech. The war having ended before she was ready to become a secretary, she stayed at home and used her skill in part-time jobs. For awhile she was secretary to Dr. Kerr at the Shadyside Presbyterian Church. Later she was secretary to Dr. Cole at Shadyside Academy.

Mark, who was a delicate little boy, had a somewhat different schooling from his sisters'. He did not enter the Osceola School until he was eight, but since Mother had taught him to read at home he made rapid progress when he finally began his formal education. His health, however, was so poor that after four years Father and Mother decided to send him to a camp school in New Hampshire, hoping that the outdoor life would make him stronger. The winter of 1905–1906 he was at Camp Asquam. The camp head, Dr. Talbot, was so unbusinesslike that Father took a great dislike to him and sent Mark to Camp Ossipee the next year. Whether it was outdoor life or increasing years that stabilized his health I do not know, but by the time he returned to us and entered the fourth form of Shadyside Academy in September of 1907, he was, if not robust, at least a reasonably healthy boy. Graduated from Shadyside in 1910, he entered Princeton as a matter of course, and from then on we saw very little of him at home. In the summers he took jobs—once on a playground in the South Side of Pittsburgh, once as a tutor to the Pratt family at Glen Cove, Long Island. Father's death, together with his own growing inclination, turned him toward the ministry, and so when he finished at Princeton he went on to Union Theological Seminary. There he met Ella Ross, the daughter of one of his professors, and they were married in 1917 before Mark had finished his theological training.

His subsequent career, though mainly in the Presbyterian ministry, had interludes in the early years of other kinds of work. In 1916–1917 he was minister of a small church (Louisa Chapel of the Grove Dutch Reformed Church) in Weehawken, New Jersey, while he was finishing the work for his degree at the seminary. After graduation in 1917 he was called to the Sixth Presbyterian Church in Washington, D.C. In 1921 he became assistant minister of the First Presbyterian Church in Warren, Ohio.

Charles, when he finished the Osceola School, went to Shadyside Academy for four years. Never an ardent student, he reached a point of stagnation there that led Mother after Father's death to send him away to school, to Andover, for two very profitable years. Then he entered Cornell. A liking for outdoor life made him choose the agricultural course. Whether this would have led him into farming no one knows, for the first World War brought his college course to a premature end. He was just beginning his third year at Cornell when an irresistible urge to get into things brought him home to enlist. He was called up in June 1917, and sent back to Cornell to the ground school of the Army Air Service. August saw him in Camp Dick, Texas, and from there in September or October he was sent to Carothers Field for training in flying. When he was ready for action in March, 1919, the war was over and he was returned to civilian life.

Besides formal book learning, the Spencer children received a certain amount of education in the arts and graces. All of us went to dancing school, the older girls at least carrying their best shoes with them in fancy bags. When we reached our destination the first thing we did was to change our shoes. I think even for dancing we wore high button shoes and dresses that, looked back upon, were equally inappropriate. I remember a dark red and green heavy wool plaid trimmed with green velvet, inherited from Kate, that I suffered in. Mollie escorted us to dancing school, waited for us, and took us home again when it was over.

Adeline's and Kate's first dancing class, taught by Mrs. Slack Davis, was held in a hall on Collins Avenue in East Liberty. It was at this class at the age of thirteen that Adeline met Chick Curry.

At that critical point in her life she says that she could not make up her mind which to love, Jim Humbird or Roy Hunt. Then Chick was introduced to her and asked her to dance, and their fate was sealed. She was carrying a carnation that day, and with it she tickled the ear of her new friend as they danced. This opening gambit proved so irresistible that when the dance ended, Chick was hers for life and Adeline had forgotten the existence of both Jim Humbird and Roy Hunt. From then on wherever she went, she always returned escorted by Chick. When she started to school in the morning, Mother, looking up from her place at the breakfast table, saw Chick join her eldest daughter at the corner of Amberson and Westminster and take over her books. Annabel Baggley, who was being pursued by Cy Hartzell, Chick's cousin, held open house after school nearly every day, and there the four young people, Adeline says, "had a wonderful time, completely unchaperoned." I dare say that galloping romance, set off by dancing school, more than anything else led our parents to send Adeline to boarding school.

The rest of the Spencer girls each in turn followed their oldest sister to dancing school, but having no carnations they did not instantly win their men. None of them learned much about dancing. Kate in her first class picked up dance steps quickly and could dance them solo at furious speed, but when asked to slow down and analyze the steps she was lost. Always, she said, she was the last to learn. By the time Charles and Elizabeth were ready for lessons, Mrs. Varker had succeeded Mrs. Slack Davis, and the Winchester School gymnasium was the scene of their cavortings. Elizabeth says that her introduction to dancing school was very unhappy. Later in Mrs. Varker's class her chief memory is of poor stuttering Emery Brenneman, who never succeeded in asking a girl to dance. He would present himself before a desirable partner and begin to choke and sputter wordlessly. Finally the girl would say, "Do you want me to dance with you?" He would nod and then they would gyrate silently about the room. Charles's chief memory is that no one ever taught him to dance. It was not the fault of our parents, however, that we did not become accomplished dancers. They conscientiously performed their duty to all seven of us.

They tried with equal conscientiousness to turn their daughters at least into musicians. Adeline, Kate, and I all began our musical careers with Miss Angelina E. Rogers. She was a tall, impressive looking woman with gray hair. I thought she was as old as the hills, but I don't suppose she really was. She lived in the old East End Hotel on Penn Avenue across from the triangle at Point Breeze. We made the journey from our house to the hotel on our bicycles or by streetcar and then toiled up several flights of stairs to her room. It was a big square corner room full, as I remember it, of pianos, claviers, and metronomes. I must have been a very small girl when Miss Rogers began to instruct me. What I chiefly remember about those lessons is my own shortcomings. Every week she wrote down carefully in a little memorandum book what she wished me to practice before I came to see her the next time. Every week I carried the little book home with me, put it in the drawer of the music cabinet in the parlor for safekeeping, and never looked at it again until I started off for my next lesson. Practicing consisted chiefly of getting up every five minutes to look at the dining room clock. Always on my way to my music lessons I would suddenly remember that I had forgotten to cut my finger-nails, and then I would frantically try to bite them off so that the nails would be of the length Miss Rogers demanded. When I got to her room she put me through my paces and must very soon have discovered how little heed I had paid to her instructions. I always hated the exercises she made me play on the clavier; its soundless-ness was somehow intimidating. The noisy ticking of the metro-nome was just as irritating in its way. Exercises designed I think for training my ear were more fun, but take them by and large I did not find music lessons very enjoyable.

In spite of myself I must have learned something, for peri-odically Miss Rogers gave recitals at which I had to play. There was a pupil named Paul(?) Matthias, whom she doted upon, I dare say because he had talent and practiced. Raymond and Mary Hilliard, who in those days lived with their grandmother just across the street from the East End Hotel, were fellow students. We all suffered together at the recitals.

After awhile my music lessons came to an end—before I was old enough to have learned very much. I suppose it was felt that having acquired the fundamentals, I could wait for more lessons until I was older and there might be more cash in the family treasury.

Mark and Charles had far less musical training than their sisters. I suppose our parents felt that boys could dispense with graces that in those days were essential only for girls. Mother taught Mark to read music and to pick out tunes on the piano, but Charles did not have even this amount of teaching. The only instruction he ever had was mandolin lessons at Cornell. Because he was taking lessons and had bought a mandolin from the coach and because he had the good fortune to possess a tuxedo, he made the Cornell Mandolin Club, but he couldn't play the mandolin, he says.

Adeline, Kate, and I had some training in singing as well as in piano playing. How it came about I do not know, but as children we three for some time attended James Stephen Martin's choral class. Though I remember clearly the room in which the class met, I have no recollection whatever of how we were instructed and what we sang. My only vivid memory is of Kate's and my walking home after the class was over escorted by Stephen Thaw who gave us a horribly graphic account of a man without arms who with his toes played the piano, wrote, and managed his feet so well that he didn't miss his hands at all.

Much later, in boarding-school days I studied singing in Philadelphia with Mrs. Jenkins, a friend of Aunt Ethel Acheson's. Unskilled at the piano and horribly shy, I achieved very little as a singer. Adeline by temperament and talent was better able to profit from the lessons she took with Mrs. Jenkins during her Bryn Mawr days. After her marriage she studied in Pittsburgh with Madame Fitz-Randolph. Undeterred by many children, she would sit at the piano, gently pushing creeping babies from the pedals as she practiced, while bigger children shouted and screamed about her. Elizabeth too studied for several years with Madame Fitz-Randolph. Not yet married, she was able to practice more easily than her older sister but I am sure got no greater pleasure from her lessons. Most of us had a natural love of music that we inherited from Father. Though none of us achieved very much, we learned enough to make music one of the continuing pleasures of life.

Adeline was the only one with any artistic talent, and this was at least briefly cultivated at the Pittsburgh School of Design. Our parents must have sent her there because they realized she had some ability, but whether it was natural talent or the result of teaching, her skill with pencil and brush seemed to her younger brothers and sisters quite remarkable. Gibson Girls done with pen and India ink, Dutch boys and girls in wooden shoes standing on dykes—these themes were particularly popular. What Adeline learned at the School of Design, though it did not turn her into a professional artist, stood her in good stead in later years when as a dealer in antiques she was called upon to paint and decorate furniture.

Father kept a faithful account of what it cost him to educate his children. Since in this day of soaring costs it may interest his descendants to know what he paid for our schooling, I am including a summarized list of educational expenses.

1888–1899	Alinda School	$225.00

This sum must have included kindergarten for at least four children and Adeline's year in the school proper.

1898–1899	School of Design	40.00
1898–1899	Miss Thurston's School	246.23
1899–1903	Pennsylvania College for Women (Preparatory)	
1899–1901	Adeline and Kate	350.23
1901–1903	Kate	218.57
	Total	$568.80

1903–1906	Miss Gleim's School	
1903–1904	Kate and Ethel	$ 402.95
1903–1906	Ethel	511.18
1904–1905	Shadyside Academy	195.00

91

1905–1906	New Hampshire camps,	
	winter and summer	1056.83
1901–1902	Baldwin School	841.20
1902–1904	Bryn Mawr College	1048.23
1904–1905	Miss Wright's School (Kate)	874.71

During boarding-school and college days Adeline and Kate were given an allowance each of $10.00 a month. I received only $5.00 a month, but I went to boarding school for two years!

Dancing School:

March, 1898	$10.00
January, 1899	10.00
December, 1900	24.00
November, 1901	12.00
February, 1902	12.00
November, 1902	12.00
February, 1903	12.00
January, 1904	12.00

The cost of dancing school appears to have been $10 to $12 each for a term.

Music lessons:

Miss Rogers	1898	$ 88.75
	1899	$110.25
	1900	$ 88.60
	1901	$ 63.85
	1902	$ 20.00

These figures must have covered the cost of lessons for two or three children.

Professor Gittings	1905	$ 20.00

Religion

Life moved at an even pace in our youth; the weeks, the months, the years were an orderly routine, as I suppose they still are in well regulated families. School and play that filled six days of the week gave way every seventh day to the special routine of Sunday. How very different that was from the routine of school days and the joyful abandonment to play of Saturdays few twentieth-century children can imagine. The Spencer children were not allowed to play at all on Sundays; all the normal joys of the other six days of the week had to be put aside: we could not visit our friends or ride our bicycles, or play cards, or sew, or do anything that was primarily fun. We were not allowed even to do our lessons on Sunday. During my adolescence I used invariably to postpone until the last minute writing the theme that was due on Monday, and every Sunday evening there was a battle. Mother, torn between her feeling that such work belonged to weekdays and reluctance to let her child go to school unprepared, sometimes let me break the Sabbath, but always with disapproving reluctance. Having spent six days toiling for her big family, she could never quite understand why we did not welcome a seventh day of rest. Her favorite hymn, "O day of rest and gladness, / O day of joy and light," she sang with the fervor of complete belief. Her own need of relief from toil added to her religious inheritance made Sunday in our family not a day like other days; the austerity of Scottish Presbyterianism clouded its brightness.

Since only three houses stood between us and the Shadyside Presbyterian Church, nothing but illness ever kept us at home on Sundays. Mother was the moving force behind our churchgoing. Father, though he approved theoretically of religious observances, seldom went to church himself, as a rule only on Communion Sundays. While the rest of us were at church he was at home preparing his photographic equipment, so that when we came home he could lure unwilling victims into his studio. Mother viewed his defection with a tolerance that did not extend to her children; we *had* to go to church, and attendance began very early. When Charles and Elizabeth at four begged to be allowed to go, Mother said, as she had earlier said to me about school, that they might go if they wanted to but that if once they started, they would have to continue; and so at four years of age they became regular, if reluctant, churchgoers. The fact that each child in turn as he began his churchgoing was restless and talkative in no way weakened Mother's resolution to bend the twig in the right direction.

She gave the restless ones pencils and church bulletins to scribble on in order to keep them quiet. Sometimes the pictures that resulted or the comments written on the margins started the whole row of children to giggling and the pew to rocking, but Mother's quiet hand and gentle shushes usually restored order. No matter how greatly early church attendance increased her own difficulties, she never let us stay at home unless sneezes, coughs, or fever rendered us a real menace to the community.

No effort was made by the minister to interest the children in the congregation; they were expected to take a fare designed for adults and endure it as best they could. Looking back on those Sunday services, I think they must have been an endurance test for adults too. No concessions were made to beauty; the Puritan distrust of anything pleasing to the senses kept the church ugly and the services austere. The walls were painted in unattractive colors with decorations stenciled in gold, and ugly stained glass windows let in a little subdued light. The pews faced masses of hideous golden oak woodwork. At the centre of an elevated, rather narrow platform stood an oak pulpit with a high-backed oak chair behind it for the minister and a chair at each end for visiting clerics. Behind and above this platform was the organ loft, where a choir consisting of a tenor, a bass, a contralto, and a soprano led the congregational singing and sang offertory anthems. Since they wore their own Sunday clothes, their costumes offered the only visual entertainment that church afforded. We often found the choir ladies' hats a subject for ribald mirth. Behind the choir the organ pipes rose to the distant ceiling—rows of painted pipes shaped rather like elongated cigars with slits in them like the slits in our penny banks at home. When we had speculated about the purpose of the slits, counted the pipes, and considered the ladies' hats, we had exhausted all the possibilities of entertainment and had to settle down to enduring the endless sermon preached by white-headed Dr. Holmes, who stood at the pulpit in black frock coat talking endlessly, sometimes to the congregation and sometimes to the Almighty. I think that he and the bearded elders of my childhood would turn in their graves if they knew how the church had been beautified and the services mellowed. The enlarged choir in red robes and caps, the minister in black gown with brilliant hood, the musical responses—these things would have seemed to them the betrayal of their religion, a wicked return to popery.

Though the church of our childhood had the plainness of complete orthodoxy, it was sadly lacking in Christian charity. I think even the children were subconsciously aware of underlying antagonisms. It was a church notorious for driving out its ministers. Hardly had a new minister been installed before the baiting began. Mother, who had been brought up to speak no ill of the minister, was outraged at the treatment accorded to the men who had the misfortune to be called to our church and always took their part. Even when she did not care about their preaching she stood up for them and ordered her children to let no word of criticism cross their lips. These orders caused me considerable embarrassment. When I went to see Ruth Edwards, Mrs. Edwards always asked me whether my parents liked the minister. I knew they supported him out of loyalty and not out of liking, yet brought up not only to be loyal to the preacher but also to be truthful, I did not know how to answer and could only mutter unconvincingly that I did not know.

Perhaps it was partly the underlying atmosphere of dissension that made church so hard to bear, but there was not even that element of interest to make Sunday School endurable. We were allowed to miss it no more than we were allowed to miss church. In the early days Sunday School began at two o'clock, though in later years I think it preceded church. Throughout my childhood at least there was only time for a sketchy lunch between church and Sunday School. We met in the chapel in groups divided according to age and were taught by maiden ladies of what seemed to us advanced years or by young girls who knew nothing. One flighty young thing, Mother discovered to her horror, was reading *Elsie Dinsmore* to Mary's class instead of teaching them the lesson. Since Mother regarded *Elsie Dinsmore* as morbid and sentimental, she had always kept it from us, and this desecration of the Sabbath upset her deeply. When the twins were at the beginning of their Sunday School careers, Miss Kennard, a trained kindergartner, taught the "Infant Department" effectively, but she was succeeded by Miss Seymour, who, though kind and well meaning, lacked sense. Even the "infants" were aware of this fact, and when she forced them to sing "Jesus wants me for a sunbeam" they thought Sunday School was silly. Mother, disturbed by the general inadequacy of the teaching, in time organized a "Junior Department" that under her very competent direction brought about considerable improvement in the quality of instruction, but most of her own children were too old by that time to benefit.

I suppose we must have learned something in Sunday School, for it is certainly from those early years that most of my knowledge of the Bible comes. What I chiefly remember, however, is racing though the Westminster Catechism trying to recite it faster than Gertrude Holmes. We had to learn it section by section, Sunday after Sunday; and we rattled off its statements of faith with great glibness and complete lack of understanding. I can still recite the Presbyterian definition of God and explain that the chief end of man is to glorify God and enjoy him forever, but at the time I committed it to memory, the Westminster Catechism was just a collection of words to me.

Mr. Pitcairn, the superintendent, was not an inspiring figure. Often he made us giggle, as when on one occasion reading the names of graduates from one department to another, obviously without having looked at it in advance, he read one name as Furry Tadpole—or so all the irreverent Spencers interpreted his mumblings. He gave out the hymns, which we sang with great gusto. They were usually Gospel hymns: "When the Roll Is Called up Yonder," "Let the Lower Light Be Burning," "Bringing in the Sheaves," "Nothing But Leaves," "Oh, Beulah Land," and the like. Sometimes there was a solo. Miss Hawes, our missionary to China, home on leave, would sing "Jesus Loves me" through her nose in Chinese. My whole view of missionaries was unfavorably colored by this performance. After the singing ended and Sunday School was over we could draw books from the library. Though generally pious tales, they were more entertaining than either the lesson or the catechism.

The only other entertainments that Sunday School offered

were a Christmas party, an occasional "sociable," and the Sunday School picnic. All I remember of the Christmas celebration is vaguely that there was a play, followed by the arrival of Santa Claus with a great pack on his back, which on being opened revealed a box of candy for each child in the audience. The "sociables" were parties for older children held on weekday evenings, get-togethers that I do not think we often attended. The Sunday School picnic, however, we attended regularly, more from a sense of duty on Mother's part than from pleasure on ours. A long train ride to Idlewild Park, a too-long day of riding on merry-go-rounds and swan boats made little appeal to us. Even these well-intentioned efforts to enlist our interest failed to make Sunday School a vital part of our life.

After Sunday School on Sunday afternoons we went home to a four o'clock dinner, followed by a period devoted to memorizing passages of Scripture. I can see myself as a not very old little girl curled up on a chair in the parlor committing to memory such words as these:

Remember now thy Creator in the days of thy youth, while the evil days come not, nor the years draw nigh when thou shalt say, I have no pleasure in them.

I liked the sound of the words, though I had very little idea what they meant. I remember being particularly puzzled by the grinders that ceased to grind because they were few. Mother stoutly maintained that it didn't matter whether I understood or not; that if my memory were charged with good things I should be glad someday that I had wriggled rebellious in the parlor on Sunday afternoons learning memorable words. And perhaps she was right, for I still remember them.

At grandfather's house Bible reading was part of the evening routine. Drawing up our chairs in a circle, each of us in turn read a verse until we had completed the chosen chapter. This, however, was not part of the Spencer tradition, perhaps because there wasn't time before the evening service, which Mother always attended, usually accompanied by the older children. This ordeal was not required of the small fry; they could stay at home and play the Bible game, which was the only game we were allowed to play on Sunday. It consisted of small cards on which were printed such questions as these: How old was Josiah when he began to reign? (I have quite forgotten what his significance was, but I still remember that he was eight years old.) Who were the parents of Moses? (I have forgotten many more important facts, but I still remember the names of Amram and Jockebed.) Who were the first man and woman? When the twins, still little more than infants, first began to play the Bible game, their ignorance was so comprehensive that they could not answer even this easiest of all questions. The rest of us screamed with laughter when they were unable to name Adam and Eve. If the Bible game was intended to induce a mood of piety, it failed completely. All the fun that a long day of church and Sunday School going had eliminated we made up for when we played that game with secular high spirits.

The only other part of Sunday that was pleasant was hymn singing. Sometime between the four o'clock dinner and prayer meeting Mother sat down at the piano and played hymns. In her childhood it was so little permissible to play them on the piano on Sunday that when she was seven years old her parents gave her a little organ so that there could be hymn singing. Many years later when I visited Miss Forman (my sister-in-law Ella's "wee Auntie") in Edinburgh I saw in her house an organ so like Mother's that I told her about it. She laughed and said that when she was young it was not permissible in Scotland to sing hymns with even organ accompaniment. Mother's playing hymns on the piano must therefore have represented a daring break with Presbyterian tradition. I am thankful that she broke it, for we all loved the Sunday sings. But most of the memories connected with the Sundays of our childhood are bleak; as Charles said when I asked him what he remembered of Sunday, "It was a horrible day."

Looking back on the deadly boredom we endured on Sundays, I find it hard to understand how any of us when the proper time came were prevailed upon to become members of the church, yet "joining the church" was a part of the ritual that none of us escaped. When we were eleven or twelve years old, we were expected suddenly to see the light, make our "profession of faith," and become active members of an organization in which we had up to this point taken merely a passive or rebellious part. How the light was supposed to come I do not know, for there were no preparatory classes to enlighten us. But at eleven or twelve something or someone began to stir us up; one person said she was going to join the church and the rest of us followed after. I know that I for one had no more idea than a baby what I was doing. The catechism that I could recite glibly from beginning to end meant nothing to me; I had no understanding of Christian theology and no faith to profess. Fear, I am sure, played no part in this matter, for neither at home or in Sunday School was the idea of damnation emphasized. I never remember being threatened with hell fire. In our family we were expected to do what was right simply because it was right; no rewards were offered for virtue. Punishment was meted out here and now, not in hell. I do not think that our generation had the morbid fear of the hereafter that afflicted earlier generations. But if we were brought into the church without fear, we were brought into it also without any solid foundation of faith. The only preparation we had for our admission to the church was a meeting with the bearded elders, about which I have no recollection whatever except that we were ushered into the Session room to meet them by Mr. Renshaw. The only difference that joining the church made in our lives was that thereafter we had to go to church on Communion Sunday as well as on all other Sundays. Before that, as nonmembers, we had been allowed to stay at home.

Church sometimes cast its shadow even on weekdays, for there were often missionary meetings to take Mother back within what we felt were its too demanding walls. When we thought she was going to too many of them we called her Mrs. Jellyby and twitted her about Borrioboola-gha. This implication of neglect always made her laugh, but never kept her at home.

Another reminder of church that followed us through the week was morning prayers. Every day before breakfast all seven of us gathered with Mother and Father in their bedroom and knelt with them beside the great double bed while Father offered a prayer to the Almighty before we began the day's work. None of us can remember when this practice came to an end, though I think it must have been fairly early in this century. Probably the pressure of time was too great to permit family prayers when seven children had to be got off to school every morning. The abandoning of this custom was possibly the first recognition, conscious or unconscious, of changing times and the first indication of Mother's ability to adjust to them. It amazed me in later years that one who had lived as long as she had under so rigid and austere a religious regimen should have been able to face without unhappiness her children's repudiation of a large part of it. More and more as she grew older religion became for her a matter of spirit rather than of conformity. Though she herself never sewed on Sunday, she could watch us sew and knit without pain, and even our failure to go to church did not upset her. She had the happy faculty of believing that we were more religious than we appeared to be and she never worried about our ultimate salvation.

Dressed for church, November 1902: Charles, Elizabeth, Mary, Mark, Ethel, Kate, Mother.

Elizabeth.

Ethel, about 1907.

Adeline and Chick in wedding array.

Mark, about 1927.

Charles and Mother, about 1918.

Mary, Smith College commencement, 1915.

Our house in Marion, Massachusetts, with Chick's Packard at the front door, summer 1907.

The Keim farmhouse, Meyersdale.

*At the Keim farm, July 1899: Adeline, Elizabeth, Kate, Charles, Mother,
Mark, Ethel, George Keim, Mary.*

Special Occasions

Holidays

Our life, though unchanging in its main out-
line, was saved from dullness by holidays and
special events that gave excitement to the even
flow of our days. Some of them were recurring
like Christmas, some of them unique like Adeline's wedding, but
all of them added color to the general design. The year for us really
began, not in January, but in September with the opening of
school. As a prelude to the beginning of the school year there were
visits to the Exposition. The "Expo," which opened toward the
end of the summer vacation, we dearly loved, partly at least
because it was our last fling before the return to captivity. Its joys
were beautifully varied, though all of them appealed strongly to
the five senses. The atmosphere was a rich amalgam of delicious
odors: the nutty fragrance of popcorn balls; the syrupy smell of
taffy pulled by being flung over a big hook until it became a
smoothly shining cream color; the sharp smell of pickles. . . .
Everything tasted as good as it smelled. Our favorite booth was
Heinz's, where if one were tall enough to be seen above the top of
the stand one could sample some of the 57 varieties. Smiling girls
handed out relishes and jellies on crackers, which we gobbled
greedily and then held out our hands for tiny green imitation
pickles with loops on their sides by means of which they could be
hung round our necks on ribbons. At another stand ice-cream
sandwiches were sold, the ancestor of today's ice-cream cones.
There were other wonderful things to buy and take home: whips,

for instance, dispensed by a man at the entrance—he always got the first of our pennies; and red glass pitchers and cups on which, fascinated, we could watch our names being etched.

Even more exciting were some of the less tangible joys. I need hardly say that the exhibits of clothes, machinery, and industrial products that were the primary purpose of the Exposition interested us not at all, nor did we feel drawn, as Father was, to concerts in the music hall—really good concerts conducted by such notables as Sousa and Damrosch. We children preferred the Cinematograph, the flickering progenitor of the movies. The pictures jumped so that even young eyes were made to ache, but they ached in a wonderful cause. The roller coaster and the merry-go-round offered more conventional but always enjoyable entertainment. The Exposition, with all these soul-satisfying joys, brought the summer to an end in such a burst of glory that we entered autumn in a frame of mind properly conducive to education.

There followed an uneventful period of returning to school and settling down to work, but before school could become boring Mother's and Father's wedding anniversary broke the monotony. This very important yearly celebration occurred on November 6, but preparations for the dinner party that always marked it began long before that date. The silver had to be disinterred from the mausoleum and polished. The best dishes and glasses came out of retirement to have the year's accumulation of dirt washed away. Mother bought turkeys or some other fowl in the country market for the feast, laid in great supplies of vegetables, and baked gigantic sponge cakes. When the day of the party finally arrived, the dining room table was pulled out to its fullest extent and the extra boards that spent the rest of the year in the cupboard under the front stairs were put in place. The table was so elongated that it had to be placed diagonally across the room, one end in the bay window and the other edging the door into the hall. An enormously long white damask tablecloth, designed for just such occasions, came out of hiding to grace the table, and the best napkins along with it. When the table was set with the freshly polished silver, its glitter was dazzling. I specially liked the little silver butter plates, washed with gold, that had been one of

Mother's wedding presents. Since Father always sent Mother the largest possible chrysanthemums on their anniversary, the house was gay with flowers.

The anniversary dinner was a real gathering of the clan. To begin with, there were Mother and Father and their seven children. From outside our home came Grandfather, Uncle Mark (and in time Aunt Margaret), Aunt Ethel, Uncle George and Aunt May (later when Aunt May had gone Sophie took her place); the aunts from Edgewood, and Uncle George Reiter if he were in Pittsburgh; sometimes a stray Gordon or two; sometimes Tomma—at least seventeen or eighteen people. Chairs had to be collected from all over the house to take care of this army of relatives. Aunt Mamie always sat beside Mother so that Mother could repeat in loud tones the conversation that the little aunt was too deaf to hear.

Dinner was delicious and we ate it with gusto. It unfailingly began with oysters on the half shell—a treat that occurred only on this one day of the year. Once the fish man packed them carelessly or the delivery boy played football with them on the way to the house, for they arrived in great disarray, the oysters having parted company with their shells. Mother was in despair, but somehow we managed to sort them out and restore them so skillfully that the guests were unaware of how nearly they had been done out of the pièce de résistance. The turkeys that followed—there were at least two, one with sage stuffing, one with stuffing well spiked with raisins and currants—were so good that no one could resist eating too much. By the time dessert came (ice cream made at home of rich cream, or in later years more exciting Dutch puddings from the caterer) the children were almost too full to swallow. On the theory that water would wash down what had gone before, we drank heavily, hoping thereby to make room for more, but when we began to cough Mother refused to give us second helpings; a cough, she said, was a sure sign that we had had more than enough already.

The twenty-fifth wedding anniversary of course called for an especially elegant celebration, though I remember very little about it beyond the fact that there were a number of silver presents, among them the spoons with gold-washed bowls that we always thereafter used for ice cream. In 1933, though Father had been in his grave for twenty-one years, Mother celebrated her fiftieth wedding anniversary.

Thanksgiving at the end of November, though it gave the same magnificent opportunity for over-eating as the anniversary dinner, I remember less vividly. For this feast we went to Grandfather's. It was notable not only for the traditional turkey, but for the favors we found at our places—miniature turkeys stuffed with tiny candies. Better than the food I remember Grandfather's saying to me once when I had been snarling about something, "Let dogs delight to bark and bite, But little children never." This wise saying I never forgot, though I doubt whether it mended my manners.

If my memories of Thanksgiving are vague, there is nothing in the least vague about Christmas. It was the climax of the winter, the crown of the year. The weeks before it came were feverish with activity and excitement. We pored over Schwarz's catalogue, putting down on our lists almost every toy that was advertised. I think in our hearts we knew we would not be given things of such unearthly splendor, but it was fun to ask for them anyway. In every odd moment we sewed, painted, knitted, crocheted, cut, and snipped presents for parents, relatives, friends, and each other, and at the end wrapped them in tissue paper and tied them with red ribbon. When Christmas Eve finally came we gathered in Mother's and Father's room to hang up stockings. Adeline and Kate had each a rather thin cotton stocking on which were stamped pictures of Santa Claus and his reindeer, toys, Christmas trees, children opening presents. I always envied my big sisters their Christmas stockings, though I felt that the stockings Mother made for the rest of us really held more. They were white Canton flannel creations with red toes and red cuffs at the top, the cuffs cut in points and each point adorned with a tinkling little brass bell. In readiness for the hanging of the stockings, were gathered together from all the fireplaces in the house, the clamps and chains from which moisteners usually hung, and to these we attached our stockings. Seven limp children's stockings and two limp parents' stockings hung in a row from the mantelpiece in Mother's and Father's room when we went to bed.

We must have slept when we got there, though I remember lying awake for what seemed hours, too excited to close my eyes. I don't suppose Mother and Father got any more sleep than other parents do the night before Christmas, for the tree had to be decorated, the presents set out, and the stockings filled before they could go to bed. They were not able to make up lost sleep at the other end, for their excited children were ready to begin operations early on Christmas morning. I do not think we were allowed to get up before seven, but it was certainly no later than that when, clad in bathrobes and slippers, we pattered into our parents' room and woke them with shouts of "Merry Christmas!" When we were all assembled and ready the stockings, now bulging delightfully, were lifted down one by one and handed to their respective owners. Then all seven of us settled down with Mother and Father on their great double bed to enjoy the first thrills of Christmas. How Mother managed to find enough things to fill the stockings of seven children I do not know, but the stockings were always full and their contents satisfying—tiny dolls, china animals, handkerchiefs, puzzles, tops, all sorts of trinkets and gadgets to delight our hearts. There was joy in opening and savoring each little package, but at the same time I always felt a trace of sorrow too at the thought of reaching the toe of my stocking and finding the last present; I wanted my stocking, like the widow's curse, to go on forever. But it never did; too soon this opening joy of Christmas was over and we had to go to the nursery to dress.

Breakfast was a perfunctory meal. We were too excited to eat, but we were made to tuck away a reasonable amount of food anyway. The after-breakfast period, while we waited for Grandfather and Aunt Ethel to come down the street to go into the Christmas-tree room with us would have been sheer agony if we had not had the "Orange Box" to control our impatience. It was the second joy of Christmas. For days beforehand we expected it to arrive from East Orange; when it came a nagging fear was removed from our minds; when it was delayed despair settled down on us and the feeling that Christmas was going to be ruined. I remember its being really late, however, only once. It was always a wonderful box, full of lovely surprises. Opening Orange-box gifts kept us occupied after breakfast, though even in the midst of tearing off tissue paper and ribbon, we kept running to the window to see whether Grandfather and Aunt Ethel had started down the street. When they finally appeared we barely allowed them to remove their wraps before we made for the Christmas-tree room. There, Grandfather, Aunt Ethel, Mother, Father, and seven little Spencers gathered outside, ready to burst in the minute the door was opened. One year Mary and Charles slipped in ahead of time and greatly enjoyed their illicit preview, but as a rule we came unprepared into a room transformed. The tree glittered; lambs, shepherds, toy houses sat on moss beneath it; tables covered with presents filled the room. I was always torn between my desire to see what was in the packages and pain at the thought of reaching the last one. Christmas very early in life gave me the first inkling that joy and sorrow are closely linked. As I lay in bed after the wonderful day had ended, I remember the feeling of sadness that oppressed me as I thought of the eternity that must pass before Christmas came again.

Christmas dinner I think we ate at our house, but the general excitement was so great that I have no vivid memories of what we ate or where we ate it. New Year's dinner was also so pallid by comparison with Christmas that it too is a blank. After Christmas the first really notable celebration was Valentine's Day. Because it was also Mark's birthday it was always marked by a party as well as by valentines. When we came down to breakfast we found valentines at our places, and the postman always brought more, addressed in disguised handwriting over which we puzzled unavailingly.

The valentines of our youth were far more interesting than the present-day variety. Most of them were pretty, and many of them did unexpected things when one opened them: a fan of bright-colored paper appeared; a cupid rose up to greet us; a bunch of flowers popped out of a box. There were some ugly valentines too, notably paper broadsides with vulgar pictures and rhymes on them that, though obtainable at Fatty Schwarz's little store on Ellsworth Avenue, were forbidden to us. Sometimes there were doll-like valentines—clowns with arms and legs that could be pulled by a string, little pig-tailed girls also with movable extremities, and the like. We prized our valentines for their beauty and mobility.

In the early days the party that celebrated Mark's birthday was an afternoon valentine hunt. Valentines hidden under cushions, behind shutters, and in other likely and unlikely places were sought by an assortment of McClintocks, Macbeths, Spencers, and Sophie Acheson. The child who found the most received a prize, and all of us were rewarded by ice cream and cake.

As we grew older parties became more sophisticated. The first grown-up celebration of Mark's birthday occurred in 1908, and of it I still have Mother's first-hand account:

> Pittsburgh, Pa.
> Feb'y 16th '08
>
> . . . Did I tell you of the plan for a party to celebrate Mark's birthday when I wrote before? The children were full of a "Valentine Hunt," as for the past years; and the twins, none too well pleased when I proposed and Mark agreed to, a small party of both boys and girls to play hearts. Geo. Macbeth, Lyman Peck, Wm. Howe, Francis Sellers, and Wm. Jones were originally planned for, but the latter declined at the 11th hour, and Robt. Donner was substituted; and he an hour before telephoned me he had had headache all day and now *"a stomach ache"* and so thought he would have to stay indoors! Elizabeth who had played Hearts for the first time at Verna Brenneman's little party on Friday afternoon, had to play—Charles was dining with Rodman—and both staid up until the last guest had departed and enjoyed all the fun and *food!*
>
> Katherine Gordon was out of town, so Elizabeth Totten was the sixth girl—the others being Alice C., Madeleine, Gertrude Wood, and Mary Kebler—and she came from school with Mary and spent the night with us. Cousin Kate came in to be company for me, and Kate engineered the games.

We scored with red, white, & blue tissue paper hearts, a la Squirrel Inn, which proved a novelty and added interest and excitement. At ten o'clock chocolate ice cream with whipped cream on top was served with macaroons and heart-shaped, homemade cookies. And, then, for twenty minutes, they frolicked in a lively manner. Kate enjoyed them immensely. Elizabeth Totten is by far the most advanced of the damsels! Mary Spencer was in the seventh heaven of bliss all day! The idea of an "evening party" seemed to her the acme of happiness. It wasn't necessary for anyone to assure me of having had a good time—it was perfectly self-evident. Even Marcus, when saying goodnight and "thank you" told me with great fervor that he had had a *delightful* time!

The "M.A.H." Club of which Sophie is not a member sent her a rich home-made valentine of wrapping paper to represent the color of a lemon.

A poor
facsimile
of the production
of the "M.A.H."
spelling excepted

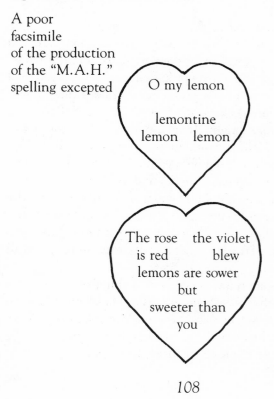

O my lemon

lemontine
lemon   lemon

The rose   the violet
is red   blew
lemons are sower
but
sweeter than
you

After Mark's birthday there was no special excitement until Easter. We looked forward not so much to Easter itself as to the dyeing of Easter eggs on the preceding Saturday. Mother bought for this purpose the cheapest storage eggs available; so in our house no one ever ate our products. Charles after his marriage was both surprised and horrified to discover that his bride meant to eat her Easter-dyed eggs. Though we could not eat ours, we loved to mix up dyes and transform hard-boiled eggs into things of rare beauty. I remember on one occasion as we were performing this operation in the bay window of the dining room that we spilled dye on the carpet and thus shifted mood abruptly from joy to grief, but as a rule Easter egg dyeing was a delightful orgy of dripping dye, slippery eggs, and gorgeous colors.

Between Easter and July normally little of note occurred except the lift that naturally accompanied the end of school and the restoration of freedom. In 1905, however, such excitement swept over us as had never before touched our family: Adeline was married on June 3. Months before the wedding day preparations began. The sewing machine whirred constantly as trousseau was whipped up by Mother, Adeline, and the current seamstress. A flowered organdie was made for Kate, the maid of honor, and a lace-trimmed white lawn costume for Elizabeth, the flower girl, not to mention suitable costumes for Mary and me who were nonperformers. The bridesmaids—I think there were eight of them—fortunately had their dresses made elsewhere, and Charles's costume as page also came from outside the Spencer sweatshop, but even so the amount of sewing done in our house during the spring of 1905 was phenomenal. Related activities added to the general busyness. We searched the town for a hat for the flower girl and then were aghast when the wedding day came to see her marching down the aisle of the church with her hat on backward! Mother and Adeline drew up guest lists, and everyone who could write respectably helped address invitations. A whole new set of activities grew out of the marriage of our eldest sister.

Mollie's room on the third floor was emptied and long tables set up along the walls and covered with white sheets. As the presents arrived they were carefully listed and set out on the tables. Since there were quantities of presents the display was magnificent, and the bride's brothers and sisters viewed it with envy, admiration, and awe.

A perfect June day made a pretty wedding prettier. It was followed by a small reception at our house. And then occurred the most exciting event of a supremely exciting day. The Curry carriage, in which the bride and bridegroom were to drive to the station, had been appropriately decorated by the bridegroom's brothers. When Chick and Adeline came out of the house and saw wreaths festooned on it and signs that said "Just Married," they switched on the instant to an unadorned carriage. In the resulting confusion the coachman dropped the reins, and when Ben Boggess attempted to pick them up and hand them over he must have scared the horses, for they started off wildly round the corner onto Pembroke Place, with reins dragging and the coachman unable to control his horses. For a few horrible minutes it looked as though the marriage were going to end before it had properly begun, but someone managed to stop the horses and tragedy was averted.

Father had arranged to have the train the young couple were to take stopped at the Shadyside station, and so they eluded the ushers and bridesmaids who dashed out to the East Liberty station expecting them to get on there. Not to be disappointed, however, in his brotherly intentions, when the train stopped at East Liberty, Harry Curry, accompanied by Helen Ayres, boarded it and went through the cars shouting, "There's a man and wife on this train," instead of the "bride and groom" he meant to say. Adeline and Chick all told got an unexpectedly exciting send-off.

Perhaps it was the terrifying climax of the wedding that was the last straw for Mother. The day after she did not get up, and for weeks thereafter she ceased to be her indefatigable self. I remember how taken aback we were to discover that she could get tired; perhaps it was our first realization that she was entirely human.

Decoration Day on May 30 brought the Civil War to life every year when we were taken to Allegheny Cemetery to see the G.A.R. march past the rows of soldiers' graves. Charles also found interesting the Boys' Brigade marching out of the Church of the Ascension.

For me Decoration Day was not particularly memorable, probably because parades were never one of my favorite sports, but I share with Charles and probably with Mark and all my sisters unforgettable memories of the glorious Fourth. The climax, the crashing crescendo of our year was the Fourth of July. In a sense even Christmas paled beside it, though the excitement of Santa Claus and presents was more permanently satisfying than the noise of firecrackers. I didn't in my heart *like* the noise; every bang made me jump; yet the excitement was worth the shock to the nerves. Preparations for this day of days began long beforehand. Father took us to Heisley's in town to lay in supplies of firecrackers, snakes, pinwheels, Roman candles, balloons, punk. . . . Mother supplied us with pieces of heavy striped ticking, which we transformed on the sewing machine into bags to hold our supplies. We stitched the bags into compartments for punk, matches, small firecrackers, larger firecrackers. Thus equipped when the Fourth of July finally came we arose at the crack of dawn to ruin the sleep of our elders. I am sure we were up by five o'clock, and from then until we were forced to pause for breakfast there wasn't a moment of silence.

Father brought for us for the most part relatively safe firecrackers: tiny "lady crackers" only about an inch long that made no appreciable noise unless a whole pack was set off at once; medium-size firecrackers, done up in square packages in red paper covered with fascinating Chinese characters that individually were big enough to make a satisfying bang; little pyramid-shaped things in silver paper called snakes that when lighted let loose a revolting brown stream that vaguely resembled a worm. It is my recollection that Father never let us have big dangerous noise makers, but Charles says that I am wrong; that he bought day bombs for us and cannon crackers too. Most of our firecrackers, however, were milder than these, safe provided no one dropped a piece of lighted punk into a full bag or set himself on fire.

Our neighbors were not limited to safe varieties. Tippy Knox had not only the small firecrackers we had but cannon and dynamite crackers in great quantities as well. One year he arrived with a large basket full of potential danger and set it down under the big maple tree beside the opening of the still hypothetical Dahlia Street, which was our base for operations. The Spencer twins, then three or four years old, squatted on either side of it watching their elders at work. And at that moment Tippy dropped his lighted punk into the basket. Fortunately Jimmy Reed standing nearby saw what had happened, seized a twin in each arm, and galloped with them to safety before Tippy's basket blew up.

Dave Reed and Tom Cowdrey, who must have been well along in their teens when we were little children, were the real noise-makers on our street. They had inexhaustible supplies of cannon and dynamite crackers, which they used to great advantage. Tom liked to set off whole packs of firecrackers at once. Into this exploding mass of red paper and noise his fox terrier would jump, leaping about in frenzied excitement and barking a raucous accompaniment to recurring explosions. The most notable exploit of these two big boys was their blowing up of the fire plug in front of what later became the McClintock house. In those days the water connection was covered by a black cast-iron dome. Under the dome the boys placed lighted dynamite crackers that blew it sky high and broke it into fragments. How the city took this piece of vandalism I never heard, but all the children on the street remember it with pleasure; it made that Fourth of July forever memorable.

When afternoon came and noise began to pall, Father produced balloons. These were usually made in stripes of red, white, and blue paper, though sometimes they were shaped and colored like animals. Father unfolded the balloon, set in place the inflamable matter at its base; and had the children pull out the sides while he lighted up. The balloon soon filled with hot air, and when it was ready Father let it sail away over roof tops into the sky. It too was a menace, with its burning mat; had it dropped on someone's roof it could have started a fire. To us, however, it was merely one of the most exciting events of an exciting day.

When night came we had spinning wheels and Roman candles to brighten the darkness. And in the sky, rockets from the fireworks in Schenley Park scattered stars. Sometimes we were taken there to see the display. I remember a set piece of Niagara Falls flowing in showers of golden sparks.

Summer Vacations

Thanks to Mother's unending activities at the sewing machine her children were more or less presentable when the time came for vacations. We were lucky as children, for hardly a year passed that we were not taken away in the summer. Father's position in a company in which transportation was of paramount importance made passes on railroads easy to obtain in a day when free enterprise was really free, and the whole family could go to seashore or mountains at relatively small expense. Even after passes were abolished travel by rail was by no means prohibitive even on Pullman cars. And so for many years every summer saw us on our way to some excitingly distant point.

The first such trip of which I have any record occurred in July 1890, when Father took his still small family to the Columbia Hotel, Belmar, New Jersey, for a month. I was a baby, too small to remember this vacation, but I vaguely remember my sense of outrage in June 1893 when Father, Mother, Adeline, and Kate went to the Chicago World's Fair and left me at home. In July 1894 Father installed his whole family, by this time numbering five children, in a hotel at Wildwood, near Cresson, in the Allegheny Mountains, for a month. Adeline and Kate, though still little girls, were old enough to take care of themselves, but I was only four, Mark was two, and Mary was less than a year old. It was a nightmare month for Mother. The hotel swarmed with children, babies howled; children whined and quarreled; confusion reigned; mosquitoes bit; and none of the young mothers got any rest. Mother vowed when she got home that if she were forgiven for this unhappy holiday she would never take little children on another.

And so for a few years we stayed at home in the summer except for visits in Brookville with the Gordons. I think it was not until 1899 that summer travel for the whole family was resumed. That year we spent the month of July on the Keim farm near Meyersdale, Pennsylvania. It was our first encounter with farm life, and I think we all enjoyed it, even Adeline, who was too busy growing up to care much in theory at least about spending a summer in the country. Mother, I am sure, had reservations about both our living quarters and the food Mrs. Keim served us. The Keim family turned over most of their house to us, to be sure, but the room into which Mr. and Mrs. Keim, their two- or three-year old son George, and a baby all squeezed themselves was a terrible trial to her. When the door was opened a stench from unwashed baby equipment drifted down the hall that nearly asphyxiated us. I think the beds in our rooms were poor, and I dare say we were crowded, but I have forgotten everything about our comfort or discomfort except the smell.

Mother was tried by the chickens we had to eat too. When Mrs. Keim needed one for dinner she would chase a rooster wildly about the yard, and when she had finally caught him she would chop off his head, de-feather and clean him, and pop him right into the pot, from which he ultimately emerged so tough and stringy that he could hardly be chewed. The butter was also of questionable quality. Mrs. Keim's handling of milk and cream was casual, and the butter was at times uneatable. But the Spencer children, less discriminating than their mother, enjoyed the spring house with its cans of milk and bowls of cream sitting in cool water, liked to watch the churning, and were not very critical of what emerged from the churn. What I remember best about the food is the breakfasts—a great bowl full of boiled eggs, enough I am sure for three apiece, and a compote full of maple syrup made on the Keim farm.

We were never able to make much of an impression on the mountains of food, in spite of being a large family. Father was with us only on weekends, but even without him there were ten of us—Mother, Mollie our nurse, seven Spencer children, and Helen Macbeth, brought along to keep Adeline from repining. The two girls, at fourteen, with skirts down to their ankles, seemed to themselves and to me at nine very old indeed.

I don't suppose that girls of fourteen were as charmed by farm life as the younger children, but the rest of us enjoyed that summer. To ride home from a distant field on top of a load of hay, to climb up a rough ladder to the loft in the barn and then slide down slippery mountains of hay, to look for eggs in nests the hens had hidden in the barn, to watch the threshers feeding wheat to the threshing machine and the machine, amid clouds of dusty chaff, separating the grains of wheat from the stalks on which they had developed—all these activities were pure joy to city-bred children.

There were other pleasures that endeared that summer to us. Another Pittsburgh family, the Orths, had a summer place not far from the Keim farm. Jewett Orth, who was about Mark's age, drove over to see us sometimes in his pony cart, and the Spencers, who had always yearned for a pony, were in heaven when allowed to drive. And then there was the circus in West Salisbury to which the older children at least were taken. I remember very vividly some pony colts we saw there, so tiny that they looked like big dogs. The only scene of the circus proper that has stayed with me is the judgment of Solomon. King Solomon in great splendor stood in front of his throne, holding a sword in one hand and dangling a baby by one leg in the other. I remember covering my eyes as the sword appeared about to cut the naked infant in two.

The summer after our farm experience we were taken to Sea Girt, New Jersey, for three weeks. This place was chosen because Aunt Lide lived there, and the Parker House at which we stayed was just across the street from her house. Kate and I had gone to Sea Girt by ourselves in 1897 to visit Aunt Lide. Actually we went in care of Mrs. McCune, who was going with her children to Spring Lake. Though we were well supervised we felt that we were traveling alone and rejoiced accordingly. The days with Aunt Lide, however, were trying. I remember chiefly that we never hung up our towels and washcloths in the bathroom as she liked them to be hung and that we never had anything but bread and butter and raspberry jelly for supper and never felt really full. Great was our joy when that visit ended. In 1900 we went there again with the family and stayed at the hotel. The Gordons came to Sea Girt too that summer, and after they appeared there was never a dull moment.

The day of the Jersey Wash brought a sight I still remember with something like awe. On a prearranged day in August every year, country people drove to Sea Girt, parked wagons and horses on the beach, and spent the day having fun of a kind that made our eyes pop. It consisted chiefly of going in swimming with all their clothes on, which struck us city folk as a quaint way of bathing. Our own swimming was done in more conventional costumes.

Whether our parents did not like Sea Girt I do not know, but the next summer we switched from sea to mountains. Grand-mother Spencer and our aunts had for some years been going to a Quaker reserve in the Catskill Mountains called Twilight Park. My parents must have been pleased with the Catskills after a visit in 1898, for from 1901 through 1903 we rented a cottage in Twilight Park each summer, I suppose for a month, though I do not actually remember how long we stayed.

I think our parents must have chosen Twilight Park in the first place because it was inexpensive yet full of nice people. We children found it dull. The patrons of the inn were for the most part elderly Quakers; there were very few children for us to play with.

Though we were often bored in the Catskills, the joy of getting there never palled. The excitement began when the trunks were brought down from the attic and Mother began to collect our clothes for packing. A great wicker trunk with a canvas cover always went with us. Its lid came down over metal loops through which a rod was thrust and then fastened with a padlock, after which the canvas cover was firmly strapped. There were several other trunks too, but they were merely trunks; the wicker trunk was a family institution. Into this collection of receptacles Mother and Mollie packed the clothes of seven children and of themselves and Father. On the day of departure an express wagon collected the luggage and took it to the station, where in due time we followed it.

We always took the night train to New York. I can still remem-ber the thrill it gave me to see the long line of brightly lighted cars pull into the East Liberty station and to smell the steam and coal smoke that accompanied them. Still better was the joy of finding our berths and exploring the drawing room. We always had a drawing room because many people could be packed into it and the tiny lavatory made easier the care of the very young. Mother slept in the lower berth, possibly with a child beside her. Two children occupied the berth above her, and two lay on the couch, one at each end, their feet meeting in the middle. Enough sections in the main car were taken to accommodate members of the family who couldn't be squeezed into the drawing room—two children to a berth.

Grown-ups never seemed to like their beds on trains, but we loved everything about them: the dear little hammock for shoes that hung across the windows, the buttons that turned lights on and off, the curtains that buttoned and unbuttoned to insure privacy, the window shades that could be pushed up enough to let us watch the glow of coke ovens as the train flew along through the darkness. It was a bitter disappointment to the child who had to sleep in an upper berth, though the joy of climbing into it on a neat little ladder almost made up for lack of windows through which to look at the night.

When we got off the train the next morning new delights awaited us. First there was breakfast in the Jersey City station restaurant. Then followed the joy of crossing the river in a ferry-boat and getting off in New York on the other side. Father would then pack us into a horse car that jogged along by the docks until we reached the Hudson River Day Line pier. There we boarded one of the Day Liners that took us as far as Kingston, at which point we changed to a narrow-gauge railroad that carried us to Haines Falls. At the Haines Falls station a many-seated horse-drawn vehicle met us and slowly pulled us up the mountain to Squirrel Inn. How our parents had the courage to take their children on that ghastly trip year after year I do not know.

Much more exciting was the summer of 1907 that we spent in Marion, Massachusetts. Someone thought that it would be fun for the Currys, the Achesons, and the Spencers to go away together. So Uncle Mark and Mother spent a weekend in the spring spying out places on the Massachusetts coast. They found a suitable house in Marion right on the harbor, and to it by degrees the three families drifted: Mark and Margaret Acheson and Mark III, a child of about two; Adeline and Chick and their eighteen-month-old

Henry; Mother and Father and their seven children; and for awhile Aunt Ethel and Sophie Acheson, I think. I don't believe the other cottagers ever got used to the hordes of people that poured out of our house! Of course there were not enough rooms to go round; what there were were parceled out with scrupulous fairness to the grown-ups and babies and the leftover children were consigned to the attic. Fortunately it was a big enough attic to make a good dormitory, with beds for the girls at one end and for the boys at the other.

The Bullivants (Leslie was a classmate of mine at boarding school) lived across the harbor; the Dows (Marion Dow was another classmate) lived next to us; and Walter Damrosch and family lived across the road and shared our dock. There were companions outside the home for everyone who wanted them and a never-failing supply within our own bulging walls. Moored to the float was a rowboat with a sail, the good ship Crusoe; and a small motor boat, the Jenissa, owned jointly I think by Father and Chick, was attached to a mooring nearby. None of us knew much about rowing, sailing, or motorboating, but we had hilarious fun learning. The arrival of the admiral (Uncle George Reiter) in his lighthouse tender added an exotic touch to our adventures at sea. On land Chick's Packard was always ready to take us for drives, the ladies enveloped in veils and dusters to protect them from the incredible dust of the roads.

Everybody had fun that summer except Mother and Henry. When the plan for the three families to share a house was conceived, Mother meant to take Amanda, our cook, with us to do the cooking. But when the time for departure came Amanda was in the hospital here with typhoid fever. We had to go to Marion with only one maid, Bertha Tretow, and import an accommodator from Boston for part of the time. Mother planned meals, purchased food, and kept the family going. I think that summer must have worn her out. It unquestionably wore out eighteen-month-old Henry. He was our first nephew and we all adored him. Every time any one of us passed his play pen we stopped to chuck him under the chin, kiss him, teach him to talk. At the end of the summer he had a nervous breakdown!

After that summer of 1908 there were no more summers away from home for awhile. Father grew increasingly unwell and either went away for vacations by himself or with Mother. The rest of us stayed at home or visited friends and relations. In 1912 while I was in Germany with Aunt Ethel there was another summer at the seashore. Father took a house once again in Sea Girt, New Jersey, and there all available members of the family spent the month of August. It was not destined to be a happy month. Father became ill and had to be taken to the hospital in Long Branch. There he died on August 29 of a ruptured appendix, and with his death a chapter of life ended for all of us.

No account of our summers would be complete without mention of Brookville. It has not figured so far in my account of holidays, not because it was unimportant, but because our visits there were different from our family vacations in distant parts. Aunt Kate Gordon kept open house all the year round, and our visits to her in Brookville might occur at any time of the year, and anyway they had a totally different flavor from our vacations in the mountains or at the seashore. Old letters of Father to his mother and sisters suggest the frequency of our visits—perhaps visitations would be a more accurate word, for we often arrived in full force. "Took family to Brookville," says Father in June 1888. "Came home Monday A.M. It is a beautiful country spot." (It was a small family then, only Adeline, Kate, and our parents.) In May 1890 he writes, "Have been to Brookville to bring the family home." (By that time, there were three children.) July 1893 he says, "Mary and children to Brookville." (Mark in 1892 brought the family to four. However, since Father adds to this entry, "Children sleeping at their Grandfather's. Don't miss their mother quite so much with this arrangement," I take it that we didn't descend upon Aunt Kate this time en masse). Mother must have been very pregnant, for Mary was born in September of 1893. On June 17, 1896, Father notes "Mary, Ethel, Mark, and little Mary to Brookville." And so it went through the years until we were grown up. Somehow Aunt Kate managed to stow us all away in her elastic house no matter how many came, just as Grandfather's house stretched to receive the Gordons when they arrived in Pittsburgh for a visit.

119

Although Brookville is only about eighty-five miles northeast of Pittsburgh the journey before there were automobiles and good roads was laborious. In the early days we had to go to town to board the train. Later the Brilliant cut-off sent it out of Pittsburgh on the main line, so that we were able to get on at the more convenient East Liberty station. Then followed what seemed to us an endless journey to Red Bank, where we changed to the Low Grade Division that followed the Red Bank Creek into Brookville. At Red Bank we had to cross the tracks in front of a puffing engine that always terrified me. Once Adeline dropped her suitcase on the tracks in front of it; everything fell out, and the engine had to wait until she had picked up the far-flung contents before it could continue on its way. Kate also once had a sad adventure at Red Bank. It was raining when the family got off the train, and in the confusion poor little Katie got lost. Drenched with rain and with tears streaming she ran wildly round and round the station until some member of the family retrieved her.

Except for these minor misfortunes none of us have anything but happy memories of Brookville; we always had a glorious time there. The first reason that our visits were so pleasant was that we had plenty of companions. There was a Gordon for almost every Spencer: Marcus and Kate were nearly of an age; Mary was six months younger than I; Bruce and Mark were contemporaries; and Caddy was close enough in age to the twins to be companionable. There was plenty of ground about the house for hiding and chasing games, and the air was constantly rent by the yells of children. The Gordons were an imaginative lot, always inventing new games and adapting old ones to current needs, and there was never any lack of excitement indoors or out during our visits.

As we grew older social life became a pleasant part of the entertainment: tennis, baseball games, picnics, and dances made our visits a round of active pleasures. My first lesson in democracy came to me there when I met at the dances boys who by day officiated at the soda fountain in the drugstore or sold us groceries. In the snobbish district in which we grew up in the city, social lines were sharply drawn, and the democratic mixing in Brookville astonished me.

Our Mother

Our summer travels and our sojourns in Brookville, though we greatly enjoyed them, were
after all only embroidery upon the solid texture
of life. What was preeminently important was
our life at home, and it was happy. I know that
time tends to make one forget the sorrows of childhood and to
idealize the past, but even so the Spencers are so unanimous in
their feeling about their early years that I know that their childhood was more than usually satisfactory. I do not mean that there
were no punishments or heartbreaks, for when I try I can remember some of the tears that were shed. Once, for instance, Mother
asked me to wash my sticky hands and then get her hat out of her
closet. I took the hat out of its box without washing my hands and
transferred my stickiness to it. Mother spanked me. I remember
too a spanking that Elizabeth received for some now forgotten sin.
I have a vivid picture of her across Mother's knee and Mother's
hand administering what was undoubtedly richly deserved punishment. But Elizabeth, intent upon interrupted play, instead of
feeling upset by the falling hand shouted to Charles somewhere
outside, "Wait for me. I'll be there in a minute." Mother, outraged
by such indifference to punishment, said sternly, "Elizabeth
Spencer, don't you know that I'm spanking you?" whereupon tears
obligingly flowed. This memory suggests that Mother's spankings
did not hurt very much, but the fact that I remember so few of
them and that time has obliterated most of the griefs confirms me
in the opinion that we had a remarkably happy childhood.

That it was happy was due to Mother. Our feeling for our parents was unfortunately lopsided. Father was a tense, nervous man. When he came home in the evening tired, nerves on edge, he found his seven children hard to take, and we were too young to understand his irritability. It seems to me sad, now that I am older than our father ever became, that we understood him so little and that most of us gave so little of ourselves to one who was in truth devoted to his children. The fact remains, however, that in our childhood few of us felt close to our father. I think Mark did and possibly Mary, but not the rest of us. Since with Mother he came first, when he was at home we had to be kept reasonably quiet, but, recognizing our needs, she gave us a pretty free hand by day, so that we were not unduly resentful about our suppression at night.

Our affection was unquestionably concentrated on Mother; we all adored her. After her death Kate and I found on the shelf of her bedroom closet an old dispatch box full of letters. "Mrs. Schpencer she tell me dese her love letters and she read dem every year," Anna Gilchrist, who was helping us empty the house, informed us. It is true that the box contained the letters Mother and Father had written to each other during their engagement, but Mother changed so completely from the immature girl who wrote them that I cannot believe she reread them yearly. I think the "love letters" she returned to again and again were letters in which her children from time to time had recorded their feeling for her. These too were in the box. One of mine, for instance, I wrote to her from Boston in 1927 when I heard how nearly the old furnace at home had come to taking her life, and in it I told her what she meant to me. The letter from Kate that follows, with one of her baby curls inside the envelope, is another. Written when she was a little girl, it expresses how in our childhood we all felt about our mother:

May 11, 1899

My dearest Mother,

Words cannot express how I miss you.

Elizabeth and Charles are playing carpenter. Elizabeth said to Charles, "Sweetie Man, you be Mrs. Woodroe and I'll be Mr. Woodroe."

Mother and Mary with twin baby dolls, September 1901.

Mother, March 1900.

Mother surrounded by her flock, September 1899.

She asked me this morning where mama was and she wanted to tell you "somepin."

It is wet and rainy this morning and we could not hoe our gardens.

Elizabeth said to tell you that her birfday came. Charles says, "Tell her Christmas is coming."

They both send their love.

Our flowers look better than they did last night.

Elizabeth has already bonished the monogram on this paper so please save it for her.

(I love you with all my heart with all my soul and all my body.)

Mark is writing to Lane Spencer.

My lettuce is coming out of the ground.

How do you like such a continuous parade as you are at?

I should think it would be horrible!

Your most devoted daughter,
Sweetest Mother,
Kate Spencer
Amberson Ave. Pittsburg, Pa.

We all loved Mother with all our hearts, with all our souls and with all our bodies, and when she went away we missed her more than tongue could tell. In later years she said that she was afraid she had let us love her too much, that she sometimes thought we had put her in place of God. If we did, we might easily have had a less worthy idea of God.

It is not hard to understand why we gave her our unqualified devotion. In the first place she was an easy person to get on with, not nervous and tense like Father, but physically strong, with a personality naturally well balanced and at peace with itself. Perhaps Father's less vigorous constitution was at least partly responsible for her vigor, for I think she deliberately cultivated strength of body to support his physical weakness. Determined to be well, she ate sensibly, lived simply, got plenty of sleep, and was rarely sick. Will power undoubtedly had a good deal to do with keeping her well. I remember her saying in connection with Aunt Ethel, who was always prostrated by draughts or the slightest exertion, that the mother of a big family had to keep going whether she felt well or not. In any case all through our childhood and youth Mother's physical health created an atmosphere of vitality in which children could thrive.

It was the kind of good health that expressed itself in tireless energy. Mary is the only one of the Spencer children who inherited this characteristic, but we all were stimulated by it. Today reading letters Mother wrote to me in her middle years I marvel at the fullness of her days. This one is typical:

April 26th 1912

My dearest Ethel:

In acknowledging, a few days ago, an Easter card I wrote that I scarcely had time to write to my own children, the truth of which you could prove so far as the number of letters received from me is concerned! Yesterday I felt like a jumping jack! Helped make beds, so Theresa could clean; and did some very necessary telephoning; and at 9:20 went down to use some yolks of egg, left from making coffee for Kate's & Margaret's party on Monday eve—given for Al & Winfred—into mayonnaise for sandwiches for luncheon. When I was about to begin, Aunt Mamie arrived and came to the kitchen while I was at work. She informed me that I should "never leave the dressing after beginning it," but I declare it was all of two hours before it was finished! I had Spanish pudding under way, also directing Katrine in her work; answering the telephone; helping to separate Lemon & Smarty, getting cotton & dioxogen for Father to bathe the injured paw (L's), helping with luncheon, etc., etc. After luncheon made ginger drops, and soap, darned some socks, and then donned my spring clothes (first finishing a few things about my waist which had been left for a "more convenient season," which is with me, you may have observed, when I have to wear them), and went to a little recital at P.C.W. at which Mary played. There must have been some more things I think for the day was *filled,* and I could truthfully declare that I had not once "at ease" sat down, until after dinner.

In our childhood Mother's endless activity revolved about her children and her husband; it was motivated by her desire to make them comfortable and happy. She taught our maids how to cook and clean, and when we were temporarily maidless she did the work herself with great efficiency, even to digging out dirt with a hat pin from the crack between carpets and baseboards. She packed laundry boxes when we were away and trotted to the post office to mail them; she made us clothes as nearly like what we wanted as she could; she baked cakes, cookies, cinnamon buns that we loved for home consumption, and when we were away at boarding school sent us boxes full of goodies. Even in her last years she continued to do for her family more than almost any woman of her age would have undertaken. I think it was in preparation for her fiftieth wedding anniversary party that, running out of ice for home-made ice cream, she went to the nearest ice plant, bought twenty-five pounds of ice, dragged it to a street car, heaved it aboard, and then dragged it up Amberson Avenue from Ellsworth to the kitchen of 719. Old age eventually slowed her down, but it never made her want to sit still and do nothing. When we were young she was a dynamo of energy.

But even in the midst of multitudinous activities Mother was always available when we needed her. She was never too busy to attend to our needs, physical, mental, or spiritual, and therefore, though we teased her about her busyness, we never felt that she was neglecting us or was indifferent to our troubles. She had a natural understanding of children that induced confidence. Even in her last years when old age might easily have raised barriers between her and the very young, she still had something of the Pied Piper in her. Once when we made a garden-club tour of Fox Chapel gardens, the small grandson of one of our hostesses met cars as they arrived. When we stepped out of ours, he gravitated toward Mother, as a steel filing to a magnet, and ignoring everyone else, he took her hand, led her all over the place, and parted with her reluctantly at the end of the tour. Another time as she and I were waiting to cross a street in town a mother with an obviously abnormal child took her place beside us. The poor ugly little boy looked up at Mother, a smile suddenly illuminated his face, and he slipped his hand into hers and walked with her happily across the street. Her grandchildren found her a friend, not just a grand-mother, notably Fran Nimick and Molly Spencer in their very early years, and Charles Curry from the beginning of his life until the end of hers. Her children and her grandchildren loved her because they knew that she loved them and enjoyed their friendship.

This natural understanding of children started her off on the right foot as a mother. It was supported by the reasonableness she brought to her task, and by the straightforwardness, firmness, and sense of justice that were an essential part of her nature. Mother was completely honest; like George Washington she could not tell a lie. There was no guile in her; she could not dissimulate; we always could believe her. Since she did not speak unthinkingly, we knew too that she meant what she said and in consequence we knew where we stood with her. I do not think she was a severe disciplinarian. What she asked us to do or not to do was reason-able, not arbitrary, and though, like all children, we might argue, we generally accepted her decisions. The trust she inspired and the reasonableness and firmness with which she handled us gave us the feeling of security that all children need.

In consequence there was very little friction in our relationship with our mother, even when she had to deny us things we badly wanted. We lived in a neighborhood where everyone had more money than we had, and we naturally wanted more than we got—ponies, toys, clothes, trips to world's fairs. But somehow Mother managed to make us accept our financial limitations philosophi-cally, I think because she was always so reasonable that she made us understand her thrift. It was due in part to her upbringing for she was very early taught to be a careful spender. Partly it came from her own nature, for she had simple wants and no craving for luxuries; and for the rest it was the result of necessity, since there was never enough money in our house for unconsidered expendi-ture and every spare penny had to be put aside for the future of the children. Whether by direct explanation or by a kind of osmosis she made us understand her reasons for denying us things we wanted. There was a basic common sense about her whole relationship with her children that tended to eliminate friction, because it appealed to whatever was sensible in them.

Anyway Mother was always so fair in her treatment of us that she gave us little cause for resentment. She never played favorites. I am sure that she felt a special tenderness toward Kate, who as a small child had terrifying attacks of croup, as a little girl developed eye trouble and made me envious by wearing glasses, and by the age of twenty had begun to suffer from arthritis. Mother always felt that she was somehow to blame for Kate's troubles, that if she had not allowed her to eat to the exclusion of almost everything else the meat and potatoes the little girl loved, Kate would have grown up to be stronger. Mother anguished over her, and after Father's death devoted herself to the cause of improving Kate's health. The other children never resented the special consideration given to Kate; she seemed to us to deserve it, and it did not seem like favoritism. In every other way Mother treated us alike.

There were certain well-established rules that governed daily life for us all. One that applied specifically to the boys was "ladies first." It helped to keep peace between the sexes. Mark and Charles, seriously outnumbered by their five sisters, felt that this rule at times weighed heavily upon them. Another that applied to all of us was that privileges were partly a matter of age; that an older child by virtue of his greater years had rights superior to those of a younger child. When the two rules worked in conjunction, poor little Charles had some bad moments. He used, for instance, to watch with growing anxiety as food was passed at the dining room table and he saw the dish growing emptier and emptier. Knowing that ladies would be served first and the youngest male last, he feared starvation. But there was always enough to go round; Mother was too good a provider not to see to that. But in all matters involving privileges these rules helped to keep the peace.

Mother also insisted that we respect each other's rights. We were not allowed to appropriate each other's possessions; each had his own place for treasures that no one else was allowed to disturb.

Mother's insistence upon the right of private property made peace relatively easy to maintain. We quarreled, of course, but constant squabbling was simply not tolerated. We had to learn to settle disputes promptly or be punished for continued snarls and tears. It was a kind of treatment that enabled Mother to maintain firm control and that resulted in friendship among her children; we grew up liking each other.

In certain ways Mother lacked imagination and had the literalness of her north German ancestors, but she had the humor they lacked—not the unquenchable sense of the ridiculous that her sister Kate and her own daughter Adeline had, but a sense of humor strong enough to enable her to laugh at herself and not to take her children over-seriously. It helped to offset literalness and to keep her values in intelligent balance. And combined with intelligence it helped her to understand people and gave her a remarkable tolerance of views that differed from her own. And so she was able to adjust to her developing children and to accept without anguish the fact that as they matured they could not always think as she did. Perhaps her ability to adjust to us was due to the fact that however far some of us wandered from the austerity of the religion in which we had grown up, she had established in us both by example and by teaching an ethical sense strong enough to survive growing independence and to insure continued understanding.

During the years of our childhood and youth what she most firmly impressed upon us was that we must live up to the best that was in us. This ideal we often found burdensome; Mother's standards seemed to us appallingly high. In the early days she visited our school frequently, got to know our teachers, found out what was expected of us, and jacked us up when we slumped. When we undertook anything, she expected us to carry through to the end; she was strongly opposed to dropping the plough in the middle of a furrow. When we were faced with any sort of unpleasant decision she had a simple formula that she expected us to make use of in dealing with it: "I can. I ought. I will."

Her letters to me tell so clearly in her own words what her standards were that I will let her speak for herself. These two short quotations show how she tried to build up the nonexistent courage of an incurably shy, socially backward seventeen-year-old daughter:

> If you are *not* going to these dances, then no need of any more party gowns! But why not "forgetting the past," begin your "Social Career" over again yourself? "I can, I will!"

> Remember how inclined you are to sink down in helpless despair when a difficulty presents itself; but don't do it any more. Tackle anything that comes—even a youth—and "do or die" in the attempt. Having overcome my own timidity I know whereof I speak.

During the period when Mother was battling to make me take the college-preparatory course at school and I, who didn't want to go to college and was afraid of the entrance examinations, was battling against her, her letters reveal vividly her basic philosophy.

> It is too hard work trying to write [on the train] or I would tell you something of my hurried conversation [with Miss Wright]. Suffice it to say Miss Wright says you have the *brains* to get through your exams. That *if* you fail it will be because you are allowing your timidity and natural antipathy to the college idea to lie on you like an incubus. Dear Love, can't you force it off, because it is not right for you to permit anything to get such a hold on you that it prevents your doing your best. Failure is no disgrace, when you have worked as I *know* and *believe* you have done. But be strong-minded enough to refuse to think that failure is *inevitable!* "Put a cheerful courage on"! Read how Moses shrank from undertaking to rescue Israel and then reflect how he conquered his fear and was the greatest man the world has ever produced! He, too, was timid and lacked self-confidence, but the doing of the difficult thing cured him. Dear Heart, I long to help you develop into the fine woman you are capable [of being], and these June exams seem to be the first step.

129

Your "Geometry" letter was received an hour ago. I will be satisfied with Miss Wright's decision. You are well aware that it is not my way to allow things to "stump" me, which makes it difficult for me to view them as you do. Rather, with Carlyle, I would say, "The tendency to persist in spite of hindrances, discouragements, and impossibilities; it is this that in all things distinguishes the strong soul from the weak." "How like Mother!" I hear you exclaim. But again I repeat that Miss Wright, being on the ground, is more capable of judging than I am, and whatever seems best for you in her judgment will meet with my hearty endorsement.

How often have you heard me say that it is the hard things we do that count—whether they be physical, mental, or spiritual—and do one infinitely more good than the easy ones. I love to feel that I am giving my children the best possible education and preparation for whatever life brings them, and I cannot think it is right for me to listen to their pleading for ease when I cannot tell what they would not give in the future to have again the opportunity they once spurned.

Miss Wright promised to write and advise me after seeing your examination papers, but I have not heard from her yet. As I have almost enough money laid by to send you another year to Miss Wright's think you can arrange about your roommate.

Take warning from your dear father and crush steadily, if slowly, that miserable "I can't," and before you are really aware of it "I can" will be the victor. Remember "*I can do all things* through Christ which strengtheneth me."

My ambitions for you are great. I do not mean specific things, but the desire to see you bring your life to the highest point of perfection in a world where service is the test. You were conceived in love—I wanted you—and I have ever felt that that must give you a foundation—a start—which most people, perchance, lack; and so I am jealous for your best development. Have you come to the calendar leaf which says that few people know their own strength? That appealed to me for I believe you have in you elements which time and experience only will develop. In fact every personal thing on the calendar was intentionally meant for you.

Molded during their formative years by such principles the Spencer chidren should have rewarded their mother by becoming presidents of the United States, heads of colleges, captains of industry, world-famous clergymen, mothers of the year! I have often wished for her sake that some of us had achieved great distinction, though actually it didn't matter. She was not ambitious in any worldly sense. Once when a group of women were talking about mothers trying to snaggle desirable young men for their daughters to marry, Pauline Edwards said in her slow, funny drawl, "Just look at Mrs. Spencer. She has two such nice sons-in-law—and she never even tried!" Mother was delighted with her sons-in-law, not because they were good catches, but because they were good men. And so with her children—what she was ambitious for for them was character, not success. If she could have chosen from the genes of the Acheson, Spencer, Reiter, Wilson, Jones, Freeman, Wilbur, and other ancestral lines that went into our making, she would have chosen those that produce integrity, not genius; honesty, not brilliance. She rejoiced, to be sure, in whatever honors came our way and beamed over our successes, but these were not the things she was striving for as a mother. What she wanted for her children primarily was neither specific honors nor world acclaim, but fulfillment of their own potentialities. She was perfectly satisfied with the genes we had inherited; she wouldn't have changed them if she could.

Mother must have felt that she had succeeded in the upbringing of her seven, for she was inordinately proud of us. When we accused her of sinful pride, she grinned and quoted from something she once found in a book that pleased her: "Pride is one of the seven deadly sins, but not pride of a mother in her children." When she died, one of the things that must have saddened all of us was that there never again would be anyone who so wholeheartedly thought we were wonderful.

When she had brought all seven of us to what seemed to her highly satisfactory adulthood, she did not sit back and take her ease feeling that her work was done. Mrs. Vermorcken once wrote a sketch of Mother in which she made of her a dear little home-body who spent her whole life keeping house and thinking of nothing but husband and children. This was not Mother at all. I do not think she ever liked domesticity; because it was her duty she kept house—and kept it well, since she accepted unquestioningly the command "whatsoever thy hand findeth to do, do it with thy might." She had a mind that embraced family first but then reached beyond it to the world outside. While her children were young it could not reach much farther than their school, the church, and the Sunday School, but as they grew older the walls of home ceased to limit her.

She always responded to outside calls for help. For instance, she came to the rescue again and again of the daughter of a cousin—a foolish and irresponsible woman with whom she had nothing in common. When Cousin Mary fell upon evil days, when her husband had no work, when the baby died and there was no money to bury it, Mother got Dr. Kerr and the Shadyside Church to take over and herself carried food and comfort to a thoroughly uncongenial relative. She did this because it was her duty, but she did it with her whole heart and without any self-righteous reproaching.

With the same generosity she contributed to charities of one kind and another, but it was not such causes that stirred her enthusiasm. She reserved that for what seemed to her positive and constructive. I don't know how many girls she helped to an education. When her own ability to contribute financially was exhausted she appealed to wealthy friends and relatives. She personally saw to it insofar as she was able that there should be a college in Pittsburgh for them to go to. Thanks more to her than to any other one person she helped pull her Alma Mater, the Pennsylvania College for Women, through some very rocky days early in this century. We used to tease her about P.C.W. and accuse her of caring more for it than she did for her own children. For fifty years she served on its board, for most of that time as secretary. She helped to found the College Club and took a vigorous part in its activities during its early years, and for many years she was on the board of the Y. W. C. A. From 1914 on she took great interest in world affairs, and for Woodrow Wilson and the League of Nations her enthusiasm was boundless. Wilson, she was sure, history would regard as the greatest man of the twentieth century. These extracts from letters she wrote to Kate in 1918 show how she reacted to him and to the war:

Pgh. Pa. Oct. 24th/18

Katie Darling:

Rather a wail was your last letter rec'd yesterday afternoon; and quite a gloomy mail for me, as Sophie had an abscess on left hand knuckle from which she had "hacked a piece" while at Mr. Kimball's; and Charles "confessed" to not "feeling well," which letter I enclose. This a.m. comes another assuring me he is better but will be on "sick in quarters" until the Lt. marks him "fine for duty" again. This a.m. brought a note from Eps, enclosing letters she had had from Chas. also enclosed postal. Too bad Mark had to get a cold when he had seemed to be so well!

Don't "believe anything" you "hear" is an excellent motto! President Wilson is so far above ordinary mortals intellectually that they cannot understand his methods. As Mark A. says, "He is too smart for them." He is a student of Governments, of history, of International law, of psychology; and is a teacher who knows methods and human nature and appreciates that education is a process of "line upon line; precept upon precept; here a little and there a little" as Isaiah wrote so long ago. He will attain the results desired, but necessarily has to work in his own way. As I have frequently had occasion to remark, it isn't what is said often but the *way* it is said which makes all the difference in the world. Also he is above all things consistent in his utterances. I have been meaning to send you a copy of his addresses, which if you read them carefully with an eye to some special subject—say peace—you will discover for yourself. The "temperate writer"

133

recently said that these railers at the Administration were gnats as compared with "real statesmanship." The gnats will live to see the day when the world will know what some now appreciate, that Woodrow Wilson is a wonderful man and that there is no greater one alive to-day! Some of them ought to be told to go tell him how to do it.

Tues. Oct. 29th 1918 2:15 p.m.

Oh, my dearest Katy Darling:

Have just tied up for mailing to you four copies of the New Republic and this a.m.'s paper. Have meant to ask you any number of times whether you wouldn't like to change your Republic's address. If so, do it at once. Last eve I was looking over all on the library table. . . . I read with keenest interest several marked articles. These were most *illuminating* in view of the President's call to the people to return a Democratic Congress. The "Victory of Justice vs. Victory of Power" I read *on time* and several times since. Read the Aug. 3rd one before it if you would catch the full significance.

In the brief one on the President's appeal to the Senate to grant suffrage you will see how his views have had to change. Democracy is the trend of the age, in which connection it is interesting to read a letter from Flora Robinson in one of the copies—especially as Betts was telling me that Eloise and herself had been talking on the subject of "batting" societies which both think are rapidly being doomed as undemocratic. The President has a far-seeing vision and if not prevented will do wonders in bringing about a better state of world affairs. I am heart and soul a *Democrat*. I believe in the rights of the people, not the protection of special interests. I find my dear big little Betts a willing listener to all I read; says she is glad to have some one to talk to about world affairs.

I agree with you that we should have protested the Invasion of Belgium—anyone's *hind*sight says so—but do not recall a single newspaper's having said so *then*, nor a single prominent man. You, yourself, "blush to shame to remember that you once stood up for the Germans"; isn't this a "complete reversal of opinion" on your part? Like yourself I couldn't believe all I saw printed & heard about them and so it had to come to me gradually; and if to me, why not to the millions all over the land, particularly in the West. Don't you remember Mary's dismay over the war spirit so different from here, she found in N.Y. & South Orange in April 1917?

No one can read these letters without realizing not only how active was Mother's interest in the world outside her home, but also how fair-minded she was and with what optimism she faced life. As the twenty-year-old valedictorian of her class at Pennsylvania College for Women in 1883 her theme was "The World Grows Better," and in 1950 at the age of eighty-six and three quarters when she died this was still her belief. In the face of two world wars and the chaos of the twentieth century her faith never wavered that "all things work together for good to them that love God." Her happy, hopeful nature could not be defeated even by this discouraging century. To the last day of life Mother believed that the world grows better. I have never been at all sure that it does, but of this I am certain, that it is the better for her having lived in it.